Education has changed rapidly during the last decade. It is likely to continue to change in the years ahead. The New Frontiers of Education Series offers information and guidance concerning the development of educational competence in all people and the wide use of all available educational institutions and resources—television, museums, libraries, and neighborhood centers, as well as schools and colleges. Based on sound research and practice, the New Frontiers of Education Series illuminates important topics of central concern and makes them accessible to a wide, general audience.

Series editor: Ellen Condliffe Lagemann, Professor of History and Education, Teachers College, Columbia University

NEW FRONTIERS OF EDUCATION

Fateful Choices:
Healthy Youth for the 21st Century
by Fred M. Hechinger

TIME TO CHOOSE

AMY STUART WELLS

TIME TO
CHOOSE

AMERICA AT THE CROSSROADS OF
SCHOOL CHOICE POLICY

HILL AND WANG
A DIVISION OF FARRAR, STRAUS AND GIROUX
NEW YORK

Library of Congress Cataloging-in-Publication Data
Wells, Amy Stuart.
Time to choose : America at the crossroads of school choice policy
/ Amy Stuart Wells. — 1st ed.
p.   cm. — (New frontiers of education)
Includes bibliographical references (p.   ) and index.
1. School, Choice of—United States. I. Title. II. Series: New
frontiers of education (New York, N.Y.)
LB1027.9.W45   1993   371'.01—dc20   93-15080   CIP

Portions of chapter 6 are drawn from an article coauthored with Stuart
Biegel, "Public Funds for Private Schools: Political and First Amendment Considerations," *American Journal of Education* (May 1993).

To my parents, Stuart P. and Ann B. Wells, who instilled in me an appreciation of public education, democracy, and political debate (even when we don't agree)

F rom 1987 to 1991 I was a graduate student at Teachers College, Columbia University, and an education writer contributing frequently to *The New York Times*. During this time I developed a strong interest in educational policy issues, particularly the politics of school desegregation and white flight. I studied the lengthy legal battles necessary to achieve minimal integration within our educational system and learned that even when desegregation occurs, African-American and Latino children will likely be denied access to the best classes and best teachers within affected schools.

This background predisposed my skepticism toward the current political movement for choice plans that include private schools, which I wrote about as both a researcher and a journalist. If court orders, federal troops, and expensive magnet school programs could not guarantee equal educational opportunity for all children, how could tuition vouchers—slips of paper worth nothing to those rejected by private schools or those who had no transportation to a school of choice—solve what Jonathan Kozol calls the "savage inequalities" of our educational system?

Other factors contributed to my suspicion. For instance, the vast majority of vocal choice advocates in the late 1980s and early 1990s have been bent on applying an economic metaphor—improvement through competition—to the educational system. Many who call for government funds for parents who send their children to private schools lack creativity, I found, and more important, lack a true understanding of the severe problems facing educators, particularly urban educators and the students they serve. They are searching for a quick, inexpensive fix to one of our nation's most complicated dilemmas. Even worse, voucher proponents do not hesitate to cite the success of public-school choice programs—programs that differ dramatically from private-school choice plans—as evidence that all school choice policy is good and necessary.

After years of studying and writing about public-school choice plans, particularly those designed to enhance school desegregation, I strongly believe that these programs, which are highly structured and driven by goals other than competition, tell us little or nothing about the potential success or failure of private-school counterparts.

I find it disturbing, therefore, that in the last six years the policy debate has become overly simplified, focusing almost solely on whether or not parents should be given greater choice in where they send their children to school. Although the 1992 presidential election helped to differentiate between various forms of choice—with President Bush advocating private-school choice and tuition vouchers and then-Governor Clinton supporting choice within public education only—the debate still remains too shallow and frequently avoids hard-hitting questions such as who has choice, how is it guaranteed, and how is it distributed.

Thus, when Ellen Condliffe Lagemann asked me to write a book on school choice policy as part of Hill and Wang's education series, I saw this as an opportunity to help refocus the discussion on choice and education—away from rhetorical arguments about parental rights and the magic of the free market, and toward a more substantive investigation of what we want our educational system to be, and what role different school choice plans can play in achieving these goals. This book examines the "roots" of various school choice alternatives and addresses the critical policy issues concerning how choice plans should be structured to meet educational ends.

ACKNOWLEDGMENTS

What started as a set of suspicions soon became an absorbing research project, as I followed hunches, gathered information on choice plans across the country, and sought advice and input from a large network of people. Some of the information in the following chapters was collected while I was still living in New York and writing for *The New York Times*. During my first year as an assistant professor of educational policy at UCLA, I learned more about these policies and began to analyze the goals and purposes of these different programs. Creative input and constructive criticism came from colleagues, friends, and family members on both coasts and in my hometown of St. Louis, Missouri—the site of one of the largest choice-oriented desegregation plans in the country.

In New York, Robert L. Crain, my adviser and mentor at Teachers College, taught me much of what I know about the politics of school desegregation and helped me think through the impact of school choice policy on racial isolation. Edward B. Fiske, former education editor of *The New York Times*, for whom I worked from 1986 to 1991, greatly influenced my thinking about school choice and other educational issues. Peter W. Cookson, Jr., of Adelphi University, Kevin Dougherty of Manhattan College, and Gary Natriello and Robert McClintock of Teachers College have all contributed to my research and thinking on school choice policies. Susan Chira of *The New York Times* asked me hard questions about the evidence for and against school choice plans, and Carol Ascher, a writer for the Institute for Urban and Minority Education, shared my skepticism and thereby gave me moral support.

My midwestern colleagues include Susan Uchitelle, director of the student transfer program in St. Louis and a die-hard integrationist like me; Joe Nathan, a well-known advocate of school choice in Minnesota, with whom I respectfully disagree on several issues of the proper structure and scope of school choice plans; and Judith Pearson, a brave educator in Minnesota who knows the perils of poorly constructed choice plans better than any academic or policymaker. I thank all three for their input through our open and honest discussions.

ACKNOWLEDGMENTS

On the West Coast, my new colleagues at UCLA have also been extremely helpful—in terms of moral support and valuable input and feedback. Stuart Biegel, with whom I coauthored an article for the *American Journal of Education* on First Amendment issues pertaining to tuition voucher plans, has been a tremendous help in terms of the legal implications of private-school choice plans. In fact, most of the legal discussion in chapter 6 is drawn from the *AJE* article and reflects Stuart's thinking. James Catterall, Jeannie Oakes, and Lynn Beck have discussed and read some of my work on school choice, and portions of this book reflect their knowledge and wisdom.

A special thanks goes to Mary Anne Raywid of Hofstra University and Rolf K. Blank of the Council of Chief State School Officers. Both read and commented on portions of the manuscript. I would also like to thank several educators, researchers, advocates, and policymakers, especially John F. Witte of the University of Wisconsin-Madison, Peggy Hunter and Steve Ethridge of the Minnesota Department of Education, and Ted Kolderie of the Center for Policy Studies in St. Paul, Minnesota, who were generous with their time and materials.

Of course, I never would have had the opportunity to write this book, nor would I have survived the process, without the help of the series editor and my mentor, Ellen Condliffe Lagemann, who has remained an incredible source of inspiration and support. A thank you also to Sally Singer at Hill and Wang for her encouragement and patience.

Finally, I am greatly indebted to my family, especially my parents and siblings, who have always believed in me and encouraged me to take on new challenges. A special thanks to my brother, Marshall James Wells, who thought of the title for this book. And to my husband, Todd W. Serman, I cannot say thank you enough—for understanding, listening, reading, commenting, and being you.

CONTENTS

TIME TO CHOOSE

CHAPTER ONE

WHAT DO WE WANT
FROM OUR SCHOOLS?

Americans hear a great deal about the pathetic state of public education in this country, and even if most of us see nothing drastically wrong with the schools in our own communities, we share a sense of urgency about education in general. But while a 1992 Gallup poll found Americans ready to embrace bold new educational ideas, it also found them hesitant to trust politicians to enact reform.[1]

One reason for this distrust is that most policymakers have failed to articulate meaningful goals for our public schools. Instead they bicker over budgets, specific mandates, and whether or not schools will distribute condoms. When politicians do discuss educational goals, the one they most often stress is that of marshaling a competent and globally competitive work force—an important but far too limited objective as we approach the 21st century.

Such narrow thinking can perhaps begin to explain why most Americans seem to have forgotten why we want or need publicly supported schools at all. In an August 1992 *New York Times* article detailing the difficulty governors face trying to raise taxes for educational reforms, one governor noted that while campaigning for a $300 million tax increase earmarked for education, he often encountered hostile audiences, particularly among senior citizens. The governor said he answered their recurring question of why they should support educational improvements by reminding them that today's schoolchildren are tomorrow's workers, who will help pay the retirees' Social Security benefits—a narrow, self-interested answer to a narrow, self-interested question.[2]

The true value of public education in a democracy goes well beyond such self-interest, of course. But if we persist in defining educational goals narrowly—e.g., having American students score higher on standardized tests than Japanese students—the policies supporting them will continue to be narrowly defined as well. If, however, we expect our educational system to fulfill a wider set of goals—e.g., preparing future generations for participation in a fair and just society—we must define those goals and search diligently for more progressive means of achieving them. Building a consensus on any policy issue is difficult, of course, particularly in education, where the potential exists for conflict between the goals of individuals and the needs of society. Students may believe that their purpose in getting an education is to obtain a "higher-paying job," but we might also hope they're learning something about civic responsibility.

If policymakers would articulate a broad vision of educational goals and clearly define policy proposals as the means to those ends, the general public could better understand the issues and, hopefully, provide the political support necessary to guarantee the quality education essential in a democracy. While honorable people can differ in defining the primary goals of education, the democratic process cannot be realized unless voters and taxpayers are provided with enough information about the purposes of different policies. This book examines one current policy issue —the "school choice" movement—to provide a clear example of how different, and often competing, views of educational goals shape and distort policy proposals.

The disparate educational policies described in the following pages were shaped by individuals with dissimilar views of the goals of education—even though all were adherents of the nationwide movement advocating greater choice for parents in selecting their children's schools. Some of the school choice policies described are more than 30 years old and embody educational ideals few people still embrace; many more have emerged recently and reflect current ideas about the role of education.

The desire to give parents and students more educational choices currently runs so strong that it reaches across every region of the country and is endorsed by advocates with drastically different opinions of the purposes of education. Thus, the structure of various school choice programs—who can choose what schools, and where public money goes—varies radically.

Unfortunately, when a phrase such as "school choice" is used by educators and policymakers to describe programs that have little in common, parents and taxpayers become confused. Proposals bearing "school choice" or "parental choice" labels often garner broad support, although they may or may not reflect what most people consider sound educational goals.

My point in this book is not to debate whether giving parents choice in education is a good idea—few in a democratic society would dispute this innocuous concept. Instead, I examine the goals and philosophies driving various school choice programs and then analyze the actual or potential outcomes of each. My intent is to dispel the notion that all school choice plans are created equal and to show that, depending on our goals, some plans are better than others.

Joe Nathan, a senior fellow at the University of Minnesota's Humphrey Institute and a strong advocate of parental choice in public schools, likens school choice to electricity—a powerful tool capable of producing helpful or harmful effects, depending on its use. This simple metaphor can go a long way; electricity fuels everything from life-support systems to electric chairs.

Thus, school choice policy is what we and our elected leaders make of it. As citizens responsible for shaping the educational policy that will mold future generations, we should take this responsibility seriously. Before endorsing one form of school choice over another, however, we must consider the desired ends of education.

EDUCATION AS AN END

Since the beginning of the common school movement in the mid-19th century, three overlapping and intertwined goals have variously been espoused for our public education system: (1) education for the common good, (2) education for individual growth and fulfillment, and (3) education for a better, more competitive work force and a stronger economy.

In the last ten years, the third goal has predominated among policymakers and business leaders and has shaped much of our public dialogue about the success or failure of education. In the name of global competitiveness, between 1983 and 1990 virtually every state raised graduation requirements, increased the number of standardized tests required, and created stricter attendance standards. In the mid-1970s, however, many educators were strongly committed to the goal of individual growth; before that, judicial efforts to achieve racial integration and equal opportunity in education reflected a commitment to the idea of the common good.

In fact, American education has evolved cyclically, with policymakers, educators, business leaders, and the general public shifting emphasis from one goal to the next, frequently failing to achieve any kind of balance. One decade brings a strong push for more individualized, child-centered education; the next a call for higher educational standards; and the next a focus on a more equitable distribution of resources. Thus, although the first two goals have lately fallen out of political favor, it is important to reconsider them in evaluating the current focus on education-for-economics, not only in relation to school choice programs but in light of their relevance to other policy issues as well.

Recent developments also prompt consideration of a fourth, far less traditional, goal: education for private profit, which has thus far been embraced only by a small number of entrepreneurs.

I. EDUCATION FOR THE COMMON GOOD

Horace Mann, one of the earliest and best-known advocates of free, universal public education and the first secretary of the Massachusetts State Board of Education, stressed the importance of education in controlling and restraining the people so that they would not threaten the "harmony of society." Mann saw a direct relationship between education and maintenance of the social order. After witnessing Boston's religious riots of 1837, he wrote, "The mobs, the riots, the burnings, the lynchings perpetrated by the *men* of the present day are because of their vicious or defective education when children."[3]

While secretary of education, Mann criticized the teachers of Massachusetts for addressing themselves primarily to "the culture of intellect" and not to such larger social virtues as truth, justice, and love of country. He complained that educators had ignored students' moral natures and social affections. And he called for greater state control over school curricula and practices—something that the advocates of the locally controlled common schools fought successfully.[4]

The authoritarian, even dogmatic tone that Mann brought to his Massachusetts post in the 1830s had become somewhat tempered by the time he resigned in 1848. In his twelfth and final annual report on the state of education in Massachusetts, Mann focused on the moral and political aspects of education as well as the "equalizing" effect that schools could have on a class-divided society.[5] His view of moral education was based on general biblical principles, particularly justice and piety, and on what he deemed to be commonly held virtues that would lead to the elimination of crime and corruption in society. Education, according to Mann, should include elements of the creed of republicanism, which he saw as forming the common basis of our political faith.[6] Mann believed that schools should teach the importance of the electoral process—as opposed to revolution and violence—in bringing about political change in a democracy.

Finally, Mann recognized that the modern industrial development of the 19th century brought with it a widening gap between the capitalist and the laboring classes. He saw common schools as one way of granting poor students the opportunity to rise in social status:

> Education, then, beyond all other devices of human origin, is the great equalizer of the conditions of men—the balance-wheel of the social machinery. . . . It does better than to disarm the poor of their hostility towards the rich: it prevents being poor.[7]

Mann wrote at great length about ways in which individuals benefit from education, but he was ultimately a strong proponent of the use of common schools to create a better society—at least by his standards.

It is important to note, however, that the common school era, which began with Mann in Massachusetts and continued throughout the late 19th century, has been viewed through several historical lenses. Some education historians argue that the early political push for public education came from Protestant reformers who wanted the public schools to socialize the "unruly" children of Catholic immigrants into "American" culture, one in which the values emanated largely from Protestantism, republicanism, and capitalism.[8] Other historians cite the economic demands of an increasingly industrialized capitalist society as the major thrust behind the creation of free public education. A more radical view of the role of economic factors in the common school era holds that the capitalist class wanted free public education in order to train docile and obedient factory workers.[9] Thus, despite Mann's pronouncements, the exact goals of those responsible for the common school era remain unclear and probably varied from place to place.

By the dawn of the 20th century, universal public education and compulsory attendance laws were common, the vast majority of American children attended school through the sixth grade, and a growing number of students were enrolled in secondary schools. During this period of transformation, a young philosopher named John Dewey became interested in the relationship between a democratic society and its public education system.

From 1894 to 1904, Dewey was head of the philosophy department of the University of Chicago, where he established a laboratory school to test his theories of learning and child development. At Chicago, Dewey surrounded himself with a "creative community" of colleagues who were studying pedagogy, philosophy, psychology, sociology, and the natural sciences.[10] And it was within this creative community of scholars that Dewey wrote "My Pedagogic Creed," an essay in which he argued that education was "the fundamental method of social progress" in a country undergoing dramatic social, economic, and geographic change. He envisioned that educational experimentation would help society "overcome the divisions between families and schools, nature and daily life, and, most important, different classes of people, especially those classified as 'cultured' and as 'workers.' "[11]

In order to appreciate Dewey's vision of education and social progress, one must first understand his conception of democracy, which he saw as far more than a form of government. According to Dewey, democracy is a way of life and a form of association—it allows for the greatest amount of participation in determining the common good.[12] Crucial to Dewey's idea of democracy is the notion of collective problem solving through informed discussion, a "dialogical" process that includes citizens from all walks of life. For the process to work, schooling cannot be used to simply prepare lower-class students for manual labor; it must, first and foremost, educate all children to participate in the democratic life.[13]

In *School and Society*, a collection of talks Dewey gave to the parents of children enrolled in the university's laboratory school, he stressed the intended social function of the school:

> . . . when the school introduces and trains each child of society
> into membership within such a little community, saturating him
> with the spirit of service, and providing him with the instruments

9

of effective self-direction, we shall have the deepest and best guarantee of a society which is worthy, lovely and harmonious.[14]

As far as Dewey was concerned, education is a process of continued growth through new experiences that arouses "curiosity, strengthens initiative, and sets up desires and purposes."[15]

Building on Dewey's vision of schooling as a means of establishing a fair and equal society, Amy Gutmann, in her book *Democratic Education*, calls for greater democratic participation in the creation of our nation's educational goals. Like Dewey, Gutmann views democracy as more than a political process of rule by the majority. It is, she says, a political ideal in which all members of a society "are, and continue to be, equipped by their education and authorized by political structures to share in ruling."[16]

But Gutmann takes a slightly different approach in explaining the relationship of democracy to education. She argues, for instance, that educational authority in a democracy must be shared by parents, citizens, and professional educators, which she believes will result in programs that prepare children to participate in democratic politics and communities, and to define and choose among the "good lives" available to them.[17]

Furthermore, Gutmann calls for "nonneutral" educational practices that predispose children toward some ways of life and away from others. This is necessary, she says, because schools need to develop a "democratic character" in children that will equip them for deliberate moral reasoning:

> All societies of self-reflective beings must admit the moral value of enabling their members to discern the difference between good and bad ways of life. Children are not taught that bigotry is bad, for example, by offering it as one among many competing conceptions of the good life, and then subjecting it to criticism on grounds that bigots do not admit that other people's conceptions of the good are "equally" good.[18]

Another of Gutmann's arguments for nonneutral education stresses that while we need not claim moral superiority for our own cultural orientation, we do need to assert that some ways of life are better than others "for us and our children because these orientations impart meaning to and enrich the internal life of family and society."[19] Gutmann argues therefore that schools must aid children in developing the capacity to evaluate competing conceptions of the good life and the good society within two principled limits: "nonrepressive" (e.g., the guarantee of freedom of speech, religious tolerance, and mutual respect) and "nondiscriminatory" (the assurance that these freedoms are distributed in such a way that racial minorities, women, and other disfavored groups can participate in the processes that structure choice among good lives).[20]

These two qualifications allow Gutmann to support such seemingly "undemocratic" policies as school desegregation, which she sees as essential to reducing prejudice in the society and to assuring the associational rights of minority students. "Schools must be diverse enough that white children learn to respect and cooperate with black children," she says, adding that school segregation is therefore unacceptable according to "democratic principles even if it is often supported by democratic politics."[21]

Expressing the goals of education in terms of democracy and the common good underscores our collective interest in education and motivates adults—even those who do not have children in school—to take some responsibility for the development of future generations.[22] According to sociologist Henry Giroux, "educating for democracy" begins not with test scores but with consideration of the following questions: "What kinds of citizens do we hope to produce through public education? What kind of society do we want to create?"[23]

One recent example of an effort to create a more democratically controlled public educational system is the 1988 Chicago School Reform Act, which decentralized the governance of the Chicago Public Schools. Originally proposed by a citywide coalition of parents, educators, and community leaders, the state legislation stripped the city's principals of tenure and called for the creation of elected councils of parents, teachers, and community representatives to run each of Chicago's 540 schools. These local school councils (LSCs) work with principals in making important decisions regarding scheduling, allocation of funds, curriculum content, and other matters. The LSCs even play a role in the hiring and firing of principals.

Although it is too early to evaluate the impact of the Chicago reform effort on student achievement, it is clear that the LSCs have successfully expanded the democratic process of educational policy-making in a city with many poor and disfranchised people. One study of Chicago's reform act and its school councils conducted by Dan A. Lewis of Northwestern University found that more than half of the parents involved knew more about the content of their children's education than they had before the reform.[24] Another study by Designs for Change, a Chicago-based nonprofit advocacy group for poor families, discovered that the reform act had, within two years, nearly doubled the number of African-American and Latino parents and community members involved in educational policy-making throughout the country.[25] And finally, a poll of LSC members by Leadership for Quality Education, a nonprofit coalition of business and community groups, found that 87 percent of the parent representatives and 80 percent of the community representatives said their schools had improved.[26] Similar democratic reform efforts designed to involve parents and community members are under way in Philadelphia and Los Angeles.[27]

School Choice for the Common Good

Policymakers and constituents who believe that serving the common good is a primary educational goal and who want, at the same time, to provide students and parents with a wider choice of schools would probably support an all-inclusive choice program that guaranteed every student an equal opportunity to choose, and every family an equal opportunity to participate in the program at absolutely no cost. Such a plan would attempt to achieve "common good" objectives, including racial and religious tolerance. Each school would be designed to attract students of different racial, socioeconomic, and religious or ethnic backgrounds and no school would be racially or ethnically distinct. While parents and students might select a school because of a particular curricular offering or special program, they would not be allowed to choose a school based on their desire to avoid students of different cultural backgrounds. Popular educational programs would be duplicated to assure all students access.

Within such a choice plan, maximum parent, student, community, and educator participation would be elicited to create and govern schools or to help revamp a school that was failing to attract students. Only public schools would participate, and open discussions would be used to resolve problems with the schools or the choice process. Parents and students who felt they were unjustly denied access to a school of choice could appeal to the school board or an oversight committee.

And, of course, free public school transportation would be provided so that every student would have equal opportunity to attend the school he or she chose.

II. EDUCATION FOR INDIVIDUAL FULFILLMENT

Casting the purpose of education in terms of the common good is likely to make many Americans uneasy, especially those whose views are more "liberal"—i.e., tending to give primacy to individual rights. Modern liberals, including political theorist John Rawls, argue that societies consist of groups and people who disagree about the nature and meaning of the "good life."[28] The role of education in a free society, from this perspective, is to affirm each individual's dignity and worth and permit each to pursue his or her ideal of the good life within limits imposed by a liberal theory of justice.[29] Thus, unlike Gutmann's argument espousing a "nonneutral" form of education to prepare children for the "good life," as shaped by the needs of their particular society, a more liberal approach would call for "neutral" education that empowers children to construct their own conception of the good life as long as it does not jeopardize the rights of others.

This liberal view recalls the thinking of Ralph Waldo Emerson, who was critical of Horace Mann and the "commonality" of the common schools. Emerson saw education as a means of achieving individual freedom. In an essay titled "Education," he wrote:

> I believe that our own experience instructs us that the secret of education lies in respecting the pupil. It is not for you to choose what he shall know, what he shall do. It is chosen and foreordained and he only holds the key to his own secrets. By your tampering and thwarting and too much governing, he may be hindered from his end and kept out of his own.[30]

Like some modern-day liberals, Emerson warned against too much "transgenerational" dominance. Parents, he and other liberals have argued, should not train their children to accept uncritically the parents' view of the good life, but should encourage them to choose their own lives,[31] especially since the "coming age and the departing age seldom understand each other."[32]

Education for the sake of individual growth and fulfillment was the central tenet of the progressive movement in education during the first half of the 20th century. This movement was based in part on the developmental psychology of G. Stanley Hall, one of the first to argue for a "child-centered" curriculum in which schools would tailor their programs to the unique characteristics of each child. As historian Lawrence Cremin has written, "The *given* of the equation was no longer the school with its well-defined content and purposes, but the children with their particular background and needs."[33] Early advocates of progressive education championed active learning (hands-on experiments and projects as opposed to just listening to a teacher); a more democratic decision-making process within the school and classroom (student involvement in planning activities); cooperation instead of competition among students for grades (group projects); the integration of student interests and experiences into traditional subjects; and an emphasis on freedom and creative self-expression. Progressives sought to replace traditional education, which stressed learning from books, uniformity of curriculum, and adherence to a strict schedule, and emphasized rote memorization and drill.[34]

Although the philosophy of John Dewey guided many of the original progressive reforms, the movement's focus gradually became far narrower than Dewey's vision of the school as the lever of democratic social reform. For instance, one of the original goals of progressive education was to make the school directly concerned with health, vocation, and the quality of family and community life.[35] But by the 1930s and 1940s, progressivism seemed focused on encouraging self-expression and self-realization.[36]

In his 1938 book, *Experience and Education*, Dewey rebuked progressive educators for being too narrowly focused on reshaping the traditional curriculum to make it more relevant to individual children while ignoring the broader social purposes of education. Dewey warned, "There is always the danger in a new movement that in rejecting the aims and methods of that which it would supplant, it may develop its principles negatively rather than positively and constructively."[37] He argued against rashly abandoning all traditional subject matter. And he questioned whether it was reasonable or desirable to expect children to learn only from self-guided experiences:

> . . . we live from birth to death in a world of persons and things which in large measure is what it is because of what has been done and transmitted from previous human activities. When this fact is ignored, experience is treated as if it were something which goes on exclusively inside an individual's body and mind. It ought not to be necessary to say that experience does not occur in a vacuum.[38]

Furthermore, Dewey noted that it was foolish for progressive educators to proceed as though any form of adult intervention were an invasion of children's freedom. According to Dewey, children should learn through experiences identified and guided by adults.[39]

Despite Dewey's efforts to steer the progressives toward broader goals and purposes, the movement, with its narrower focus, was for the most part swallowed up by the 1940s by a more powerful group of reformers, whom David Tyack calls "administrative progressives." This group of educators, who dominated educational policy-making well into the 1950s, was not interested in students' individual needs but rather in creating an educational science—centralizing control of the schools and the curriculum and turning all decision making over to educational experts.[40]

Yet by the late 1960s and throughout the 1970s, there was a resurgence in the emphasis on the individual needs of students; this resurgence was led by radical liberals—sometimes called neo-progressives or "romantic critics"—who attacked the public schools for their inability to meet the educational needs of individual students, especially those disfranchised from the economic power structure within society. Critics such as A. S. Neill, John Holt, and Paul Goodman charged that schools "quashed individualism, ignored students' emotional needs, and perpetuated an inegalitarian social order."[41]

The argument for greater student autonomy and freedom from adult authority was perhaps most forcefully made in Ivan Illich's 1970 book, *Deschooling Society*, in which he called for the abolishment of compulsory education. To Illich, mandatory school attendance was the "institutionalized" result of the unequal power relations between adults and children.[42]

For the romantic critics, the goal of education was to help individual students in their quest for meaning. By the late 1970s, the attacks of the romantic critics had helped fuel changes in educational practices: a decline in the traditional authority of the teacher, fewer traditional academic subjects, and a reduction of graduation requirements.[43]

But this emphasis on the freedom of "individual" children from too much institutional or parental direction is not consistent with all libertarian views of education. Other, more conservative liberals subscribe to the very "American" view of liberty based in the writings of John Locke—that *adult* citizens should maintain the freedom to choose their own good and to insulate their children from ways of life or thinking that conflict with their own.[44] This focus on the "moral unity" of the family is what Amy Gutmann calls the "state of families" theory, which strives to guarantee the strength and legitimacy of parents' rights to pass values on to their children.[45] Parents' ability to exercise control over where and how their children are educated is an important aspect of individual freedom from the state, as far as Lockean liberals are concerned.

This view of the right of adults to decide what is best for their children can easily conflict with that espousing the "individual" right of students to enjoy a more self-directed education. This conflict can become most apparent when parents choose to send their children to religious schools. Liberals who argue that children should enjoy the maximum opportunity to choose their own concept of the good life would, theoretically, disagree with the right of parents to send their children to sectarian schools unless the children have first been exposed to several different religions and decided which is best for them.

School Choice for Individual Fulfillment

School choice plans designed to guarantee maximum individual choice and freedom with no constraints whatsoever could potentially look quite different from those intended to serve the common good.

Modern liberals would most likely favor schools of choice structured to meet the individual educational needs of the students enrolled. The focus would be very much on students and their freedom from parental control over what schools they attend and from adult—government or teacher—control over what they learn. Liberals would probably allow students to choose public or private schools, and would seek to ensure—by means of larger government scholarships or tuition vouchers—that family income did not limit opportunity.

Conservatives and libertarians would most likely prefer that parents have maximum freedom to choose their children's schools—public or private—with support from public funds. Each parent would receive the same amount from the government per school-age child. Those who had the money and the inclination to spend more on their child's education would, of course, be free to do so.

III. EDUCATION FOR A BETTER-TRAINED WORK FORCE

Despite the compelling nature of these other educational "ends," policy debates of the last decade have been dominated by those who espouse the economic goals of education. Beginning with the clarion call sounded in 1983 when the National Commission on Excellence in Education released *A Nation at Risk: The Imperative for Educational Reform* and continuing well into the recession-riddled 1990s, most of the attention given to our public schools has focused on their contribution to America's economic decline and future competitiveness.

Obviously, this is not the first time national leaders have articulated the goals and purposes of education in competitive and economic terms. As was mentioned earlier, there is ample historical evidence to suggest that the work-force needs of industry have had a profound impact on educational policy since the beginning of the common school movement.

Educational historian Michael Katz has argued that the "upper-class" school reformers of the 19th century sought to design a common school system that would prepare workers to serve the needs of an urban and industrial society. This produced factorylike schools emphasizing attendance, discipline, and order.[46]

Although Katz's analysis has been challenged by historians who have demonstrated working-class influence on common schools in the 19th century, the parallels between the burgeoning educational system and the expanding manufacturing industry at the turn of the century were numerous:

> Social promotion, tracking, and the rapid spread of educational measurement reflected the powerful influence of the theory of "scientific management" at the time of the expansion of public secondary education early in the century. Mass production was the cornerstone of the theory. . . . And educators sought to apply the tenets of industrial production to the task of providing secondary schooling on a mass scale. Schools were organized as educational factories.[47]

The rush among educators to mirror the industrial sector in creating and managing schools provides the strongest evidence that the mustering of a well-trained work force was one—if not *the*—primary goal of education during the industrial revolution.

As the educational requirements for entry-level jobs rose dramatically following World War II, success in the job market became increasingly tied to educational achievement. And in the last 30 years, international competition to win the "brain race" has intensified, placing additional pressure on schools to produce better-trained workers.

International competitiveness became a major force in educational policy during the early years of the Cold War. From the late 1940s on into the 1960s, federal and state policymakers pushed for more science education at all grade levels. Although science education was seen as particularly crucial to the country's economic viability and military preparedness, politicians and business leaders also complained about educators' neglect of such basic academic disciplines as mathematics, English, history, and foreign languages. These critics argued that the progressive, child-centered educational practices of the 1930s and 1940s had pushed school curricula too far away from the core subjects.[48]

The National Science Foundation Act of 1950 underscored the nation's preoccupation with science education and the perceived need to produce more scientists and engineers. The NSF committee to oversee grants and research included military and industrial leaders as well as scientists.[49] This emphasis on science education intensified in 1957, when the Soviet Union launched *Sputnik I*, the first space satellite. For many Americans *Sputnik* symbolized our inability to compete technologically with the Soviets. In 1958, responding to the public outcries triggered by *Sputnik*, Congress passed the National Defense and Education Act, which provided fellowships, grants, and loans to school districts to encourage the study of science, mathematics, and foreign languages, and funded school construction and equipment purchases.[50] Thus, while much post–World War II educational policy was explicitly aimed at educating scientists and engineers who could design the technology and weapons to help the United States win the Cold War, the overarching assumption was that the main role of education is to develop "human resources" to support a changing labor market.[51]

In the 1960s, for instance, many federal programs were ideologically based on economic "human capital" theory, which asserts that people are poor primarily because they lack the capital—i.e., specific skills, knowledge, and motivation—demanded by an increasingly tight and technological labor market. A 1964 report by the Council of Economic Advisers argued that if children of poor families were given the right skills and motivation, they would not grow up to become poor adults.[52] Educational programs such as the Job Corps, compensatory elementary and secondary education, and Head Start were central to the War on Poverty.

The focus on education for the sake of economic competitiveness and a well-trained work force, therefore, is nothing new. Like most educational policy issues, it is emphasized cyclically, when national attention turns to productivity, international competition, and—by default—poverty.

The 1980s, though, saw not only a renewed emphasis on the importance of education for economic competitiveness but also a sharp increase in the direct involvement of business leaders in educational policy-making. This shift in the role of business leaders in education policy became visible with the publication of the 1983 report *A Nation at Risk*, which presented a troubling portrait of failing schools and ill-prepared students to the American public and triggered much the same response as the Soviet satellite had 25 years earlier. Although the 1983 report dealt with both economic and military security, this time—unlike the *Sputnik* aftermath—the concerns were primarily economic. The failure of the schools had contributed to the decline in the nation's status as an economic superpower. The message was sobering, a veritable call-to-arms:

> We live among determined, well-educated, and strongly motivated competitors. We compete with them for international standing and markets, not only with our products, but also with the ideas of our laboratories and neighborhood workshops. . . . Knowledge, learning, information, and skilled intelligence are the new raw material of international commerce and today are spreading throughout the world as vigorously as miracle drugs, synthetic fertilizers, and blue jeans did earlier.[53]

A Nation at Risk was one of the first in a long series of reports released in the 1980s that would strongly criticize the educational system for failing to prepare students for the work force. Many of these reports were initiated by the business community; most others reflected the input and demands of business leaders.

According to Thomas Toch in his book *In the Name of Excellence*, during the 1960s and 1970s those whose interests were "represented by chambers of commerce did not have much to do with public education." But by the early 1980s, Toch notes, intensifying foreign competition, a more intellectually demanding workplace at home, and the devastating effects of the 1981–82 recession created a sense of urgency within the business community. Much of this urgency found expression as concern about the educational system. By 1983 nearly 85 percent of the heads of the nation's largest companies said that business should be more involved in education than it had been.[54]

The year before *A Nation at Risk* was released, the U.S. Chamber of Commerce issued a report titled *American Education: An Economic Issue*, in which it warned that the nation's schools were lagging behind Japanese and Soviet schools in terms of training workers. Following only a week behind *A Nation at Risk*, the Education Commission of the States' special task force on Education for Economic Growth published a report titled *Action for Excellence*. The task force, which included several of the nation's most powerful chief executives, including those from IBM, Ford Motor Company, and Dow Chemical, charged that the public schools' failure to produce a competent work force was undermining the economic strength of the country. The Committee for Economic Development (CED), an organization of 200 business executives, published a 1985 report titled *Investing in Our Children: Business and the Public Schools*, which argued for American businesses to play a larger role in educational reform.[55]

In addition to their involvement on national task forces, business executives were becoming more involved with state and local policy-making. At the state level, governors and legislators formed more than 300 educational reform task forces and commissions during the 1980s, with business executives representing no less than 31 percent of the membership. Still, the majority of business involvement was confined to local-level programs such as partnerships and adopt-a-school projects. "Those efforts ranged from career days and the donation of materials and equipment to complex district-wide compacts in which businesses promise to favor local public-school graduates in hiring decisions."[56]

Such programs grew rapidly in the 1980s, with 17 percent of the nation's schools involved in some project with a corporation in 1984, and close to 40 percent involved in about 140,000 active projects by 1991.[57]

In some respects, corporate involvement has been politically advantageous to educators. It has drawn more attention and lent greater credibility to educational causes. And corporate giving to K-12 education reached a new annual height in 1990—$264 million—although these funds are spread unevenly.[58] Critics of business involvement in education also note that the recent increase in corporate philanthropy for schools is not enough to make up for the loss of corporate tax revenues that resulted from Reagan's tax reform laws.

Furthermore, the educational end advanced by this business involvement is unambiguously economic, and the growing influence of business leaders on federal policy has resulted in neglect of some of the most pressing issues facing schools today. As George R. Kaplan and Michael D. Usdan have written,

> At a time when urban school systems are becoming resigned to "resegregation" as a permanent condition and when financial disparities between rich and poor schools are a national disgrace, no networks, no national coalition, no emergency committees of concerned leaders are rallying mass support for remedial action.[59]

Many liberal and radical commentators worry about the propensity of schools, especially those receiving a vast influx of corporate gifts, to inculcate capitalist values of competition and consumption without teaching children to be critical of the unequal distribution of wealth and power in our society. These critics view schools not as the great equalizer and balance wheel of society, as in Horace Mann's view, but simply as instruments for reproducing the inequalities of the capitalist system—by channeling students from lower-class families into lower-funded schools and, ultimately, lower-paying and lower-status jobs. Business involvement in education for the sake of a more efficient "Work Force 2000," in this view, is part of that process.[60]

School Choice for a Better-Trained Work Force
For those who envision school choice as a means of achieving the "ultimate" educational goal of a better-trained and more globally competitive work force, the best model for a choice plan—and for schools themselves—might be the corporate one.

Those who advocate school choice for the sake of economic competitiveness stress that schools should be forced to compete for students the way corporations compete for clients. Then they would turn out a better product.

These reformers would structure school choice around competition, money, and test scores. Government education dollars would follow students to their public or private schools of choice, and schools that failed to attract enough clients would be "out of business." Parents and students would theoretically shop for the best education their money could buy; teachers and principals would be motivated to work harder—to teach more and better, and to raise those test scores. If educators were not adequately motivated by the lure of more money for their schools, they would at least be threatened by the specter of unemployment.

These reformers might also argue for a specialized set of national standards and tests to help parents and students evaluate schools—based not on a student's individual educational needs but rather on the ranking of the school within a competitive market.

According to advocates of this economics-driven model, little attention should be paid to issues such as racial or ethnic integration, because scant evidence exists that such "social engineering" raises test scores. Extra tuition dollars for students from poor families would not be necessary, because the free-market would be expected to meet the demands of all students.

IV. EDUCATION FOR PROFIT

In 1991 Tennessee entrepreneur and media mogul Christopher Whittle announced that he would start a chain of for-profit private schools. Whittle said his educational venture, named the Edison Project, would redesign the concept of elementary and secondary education from the ground up. By the turn of the century he plans to have opened 1,000 schools with "state-of-the-art facilities" at a per-pupil cost of approximately $5,500 a year—about $1,300 more than the national average public school expenditure.

By using less human capital and more technology—not to mention a great deal of volunteer labor from both parents and students—Whittle plans to keep operational costs to a minimum, which will allow him to draw a healthy profit off the top: a projected $105 million in the first year, 1996, with just 200 schools and 150,000 students. By the year 2010—with 1,000 schools and two million students—Whittle plans to reap profits of $1.5 billion for his parent corporation, Whittle Communications.

The announcement of a chain of for-profit schools created quite a stir, but it was not the first time Whittle had shocked the nation by mixing profit motives with pedagogy. In 1989 the self-made millionaire launched Channel One, a television news service that brought a 12-minute current events program to both public and private high schools across the country, along with free television sets and satellite dishes. In return, the schools had to promise that students would sit through not only the news program, but a minimum two minutes of commercials included in the broadcast as well.

Critics called Whittle's program everything from "academic acid rain" to "educational junk food." Thus far, there is no evidence that Channel One helps students learn. In a study funded by Whittle himself, regular viewers of Channel One were able to answer only one more question correctly on a 30-item test on current events than nonviewers.[61]

Today, resistance among some state and local policymakers remains strong. New York State has banned Channel One in public schools. A California state judge would not allow the state superintendent to ban Channel One, but he imposed new restrictions, requiring that all students be informed in writing that they have no obligation to watch the program.[62] In Fort Worth, Texas, the school board recently voted to keep Channel One out of their schools.[63]

Despite such opposition, many schools hungry for educational technology are eager to sign on. Within the first year, Channel

One had brought 325,000 television sets and 5,000 miles of cable wiring into almost 8,000 schools. The company estimates that 7.1 million students in 47 states saw the program during the 1991–92 school year.[64] By the end of the project's second year, 8 million students enrolled in 40 percent of U.S. high schools had taken Whittle up on his offer of free technology. Advertising rates for 30-second spots on Channel One rose from $150,000 to $157,000 by the 1992–93 school year, and Whittle's 1992 annual revenue from the project was estimated at about $120 million. In June 1993, Whittle Communications asked Channel One subscribers for permission to exceed the contractual two-minute limit on daily commercials by 30 seconds. According to a company spokesperson, the additional commercial time on selected days would allow Whittle to recoup lost revenues from days in which it did not sell out the two minutes of advertising.[65]

Whatever its value as an educational tool, Channel One has been an unqualified business success. But the future of the Edison Project is far less certain. Critics say Whittle has grossly underestimated the costs of running a school, not to mention parents' willingness to "volunteer" at a school where they are paying $5,500 a year in tuition—all in the name of greater Whittle profits.

In the spring of 1992, Whittle convinced Benno C. Schmidt, Jr., then president of Yale University, to become the president and chief executive officer of the Edison Project. Mr. Schmidt will lead Mr. Whittle's hand-picked "design team," which consists largely of economists, journalists, and policy people who know little about day-to-day life in schools. There is only one former school principal on the team. Start-up costs—including Schmidt's annual salary, estimated at $1 million[66]—will be financed in part by $60 million from Whittle Communications and its partners Time Warner, Philips Electronics, and Associated Newspapers of Britain. Meanwhile, Whittle hopes to raise the additional $2 billion in capital he needs to build the first 200 schools from some of the country's largest computer and software companies. As Jesse Kornbluth speculated in the August 1992 *Vanity Fair*, these corporations may indeed back the Edison Project in hopes of being named the project's sole supplier of interactive technology and educational software.[67]

This venture may seem frightening to educators who entered the field not to make millions of dollars but to help children, yet it is indicative of a small but growing trend in education—that of entrepreneurs looking to make money by running cost-efficient schools. The other well-known example is the Minneapolis-based Education Alternatives Inc., which became the first company to run a public school for profit under contract from a school district. As of the 1992–93 school year, Education Alternatives had been contracted to run the South Pointe Elementary School in Miami Beach and one middle and eight elementary schools in Baltimore, and it currently serves as superintendent of schools for Duluth, Minnesota. The company also runs two private schools in New Mexico and Minnesota.[68]

Of course, neither the Edison Project nor the Educational Alternatives venture represents the first time that private industries have made money by offering goods or services to schools. Certainly textbook and school-supplies manufacturing are multimillion-dollar businesses, as are the food and transportation industries that service schools.

The concept of for-profit private schools is also not new in the proprietary education business, where some respectable and many unrespectable companies offer adults training in everything from cosmetology to word processing. (The high default rate of these for-profit schools should serve as a warning to those who see the profit motive as a good way to get fresh ideas and talented people into the field of education.)

But Whittle, Schmidt, and Educational Alternatives represent a new era in which corporations will attempt to run respectable K-12 private schools and make handsome profits while doing it. Although these entrepreneurs espouse altruistic goals—the opportunity to contribute to the future of the country—one has to wonder why Whittle, his team, and his investors need to make millions of dollars as well. It appears as though profit-making has become an increasingly important educational goal.

School Choice for Profit

Those who approach education as a profit-making venture would be inclined to lobby for school choice plans that encourage clients to spend money at their schools. Government scholarships—or tuition vouchers—with no restrictions on use would most likely be key elements. But the vouchers would have to be fairly generous to ensure that large profits could be made, even in schools serving low-income students. The educational entrepreneurs, if they had their way, would call for tuition vouchers at least the size of the average per-pupil expenditure in a public school. Extra stipends for students from poor families would be welcomed. For-profit school entrepreneurs such as Whittle would soon be lining their pockets with tax dollars, much like the big defense contractors of the 1980s.

SCHOOL CHOICE AS A MEANS

Intelligent evaluation of any school choice program or policy depends on a clear understanding of the underlying educational goals it serves. As the following chapters will demonstrate, there are as many ways of packaging school choice as there are people who see choice in education as a way of achieving a specific goal—the common good, individual fulfillment, a better-trained work force, or private profits.

Over the last 30 years, school choice programs have been used to desegregate schools, accommodate students' individual needs, provide parents with greater control over their children's education, and produce a more competitive educational system. Today, some school choice plans offer parents choices within the boundaries of a single school district; others encompass an entire state and let parents choose among more than 400 districts. Some choice plans ensure an equal chance to choose for all families, whereas others simply offer the promise of choice without any guarantee that quality schools will accept or educate students with limited money or without prior school success. Some school choice plans have broad social goals; others are defined narrowly as cost-saving devices.

In many of these plans, the educational goals that I have outlined overlap and even complement one another, and many policies are designed with more than one purpose in mind. But the size and scope of a school choice plan—determining who has access to which schools and whether public money will follow children to private schools—should be driven by some envisioned educational end.

The following chapters examine various school choice plans that grew out of different views of the purpose of education. Linking these programs to the intentions that fostered them and separating them from each other will establish a groundwork that will help parents, students, educators, and citizens to participate in the process of redefining American education. Then we can call for specific school choice policies with a clear understanding of the educational goals they embraced.

P erhaps the most misleading aspect of the recent calls for greater choice in education is their failure to acknowledge the enormous amount of parental choice that currently exists within public education, especially in large urban school districts that are considered the most bureaucratic and least responsive to students' needs. And yet students entering high school in large cities such as New York and Los Angeles can apply to literally hundreds of public secondary schools. The large degree of school choice in urban districts began in the early 1970s, when the "free schools movement" led to the creation of thousands of alternative public schools.

Reliable national educational statistics are hard to come by because the nation's 15,367 public school districts have long enjoyed a tradition of local control, free of federal government interference.[1] Information is especially scarce when it comes to counting and describing alternative schools, which often operate outside of their district's dominion or as small "schools within a school." Experts estimate the number of alternative schools nationwide to be somewhere between 4,000 and 8,000, with approximately three-fourths of these public. Yet, in an era replete with talk of the virtues of private schools, free-market education, and tuition vouchers, little mention is made of these 3,000 or so public alternative schools, which have been offering parents educational choices for more than two decades.

This lack of attention stems partly from philosophical differences dividing those who advocate private-school choice plans and tuition vouchers and those who work in alternative schools. The alternative education movement of the 1970s was based on the child-centered approach to education espoused by the early progressives and has embraced the "individual growth and fulfillment" goal. Many of today's voucher advocates, on the other hand, tend to be more interested in fostering economic competitiveness, and thus seek to make schools more efficient and accountable by forcing them to compete with one another in the market. Other voucher advocates are "libertarians" in the Lockean sense—they espouse the individual rights of parents to control their children's education and, therefore, to direct tax dollars to the public or private school they choose. Both views are clearly at odds with the alternative education stress on students' rights to attend a school in which they can thrive.

An analysis of public alternative schools—their origins, range of choices offered, successes, and problems—can yield valuable lessons for the contemporary choice debate. It can help us appreciate the amount of school choice already available within the public sector and suggest important questions about the consequences of choice plans driven by different goals.

THE BEGINNINGS OF ALTERNATIVE EDUCATION IN AMERICA

What was to become the American alternative schools movement began in the mid-1960s as groups of parents and teachers founded hundreds of private, or "independent," schools in cities such as Boston, New York, Chicago, Washington, D.C., St. Paul, St. Louis, and San Francisco. These urban alternative schools, or "free schools," provided poor and minority children—those who had been the most victimized by public education—with an educational program designed to empower and liberate.[2] While some of these schools were racially integrated and stressed cultural diversity, many were all-black and shaped by an ideology known in some places as " 'blackology'—the need to educate the children in basic skills and in pride of race."[3]

At the same time, a number of mostly rural free schools were founded by white middle- and upper-middle-class parents and educators who were associated with the 1960s' counterculture movement. These were often attached to one of the communes, or "intentional communities," that sprang up across the country —from the hills of Tennessee to the beaches of southern California to the mountains of Vermont.[4] According to Carl Weinberg, a professor at UCLA who studied and worked in several early alternative schools, both urban and rural educators attempted to create alternative forms and philosophies of education, but to different ends. As he noted in 1973, "One group demands equal opportunities to learn the basic skills for mobility, and the other cries for freedom from the manipulation of adults in order to explore self, interpersonal relations, and cognitive curiosities, whether these lead to status mobility or not. . . . [A]lternatives must be understood as responses to both kinds of complaints."[5]

The founders of these private alternative schools, both urban and rural, rejected a public educational system that they considered impersonal and nonresponsive to children's individual needs. Many were inspired by the success of English educator A. S. Neill and the alternative Summerhill School he founded in Leiston, England, in the 1920s.[6] Drawing on the theories of Sigmund Freud, Neill argued that children need to be free to learn and discover at their own pace; he also believed in the innate goodness of all children and the need to deliver them from the fear of authority. He later wrote that when he and his wife founded Summerhill they had one main idea: "*to make the school fit the child*—instead of making the child fit the school,"[7] an approach aligning Neill and Summerhill with the developmental psychology of G. Stanley Hall and the views of many progressive American educators of the time.[8] To this day, at Summerhill, classes or "lessons" are optional, and all students, from age 5 to

15, participate in the General School Meeting, where school policy is established.

Visionary educators in the United States also attempted to create private alternative schools at the beginning of the 20th century—although with somewhat less success than that attained by Neill. Established in 1915 in Stelton, New Jersey, the Modern School focused on "empowering" children of working-class families by teaching leadership and self-determination. It quickly became the nation's leading center for radical education.[9]

The Modern School grew out of an alliance of the progressive labor and progressive education movements conceived as a means of rebelling against "the processes within the public schools that were shaping individual needs for the corporate state." These educators saw public schools as instruments of the capitalist class designed to perpetuate an unequal society. The fact that business leaders dominated most boards of education and refused to "allow labor education classes" or other anticapitalist instruction was not lost on them.[10]

In 1924 representatives of labor and education founded Manumit School on a 177-acre working farm in Pawling, New York. Like the Modern School, Manumit was established primarily for children of workers, but it was also a boarding school, designed to foster a strong sense of community. The students governed themselves and learned through day-to-day experiences on the farm. Historian Joel Spring, in *The American School, 1642–1990*, notes that children at the Manumit School were organized into trade unions, and that some actually called labor strikes to protest conditions at the school.[11]

Like many progressive educators of their day, the educators at Manumit attempted to incorporate the philosophy of John Dewey into their teachings.[12] Yet, as noted earlier, Dewey became critical of progressive educators for emphasizing tangential child-relevant experiences over important adult-guided experience. By the 1940s, the progressive movement had faded with the ascent of the "progressive administrators"—men with professional training in education who shared a faith in "educational science." These administrators, who had become quite influential by the late 1930s, set out to centralize control of urban schools in small elite boards, increase rigid tracking systems in which student placement was based on standardized test scores, and disempower teachers by taking curricular decisions out of their hands. Obviously, these "reforms" stood in sharp contrast to progressive educational philosophy.[13] Most of the early alternative schools vanished with the commitment to truly progressive reform. Both the Modern and Manumit schools closed by the early 1950s.

Another reason the early-20th-century push for alternative schools dissipated in the 1940s was the rise of labor unions, especially those representing teachers. The introduction of more prolabor material into the curriculum also reduced the political pressure for an alternative system of labor schools.[14]

Interest in a more child-centered, progressive form of education outside the mainstream public schools reemerged in the 1950s with the organization of a Summerhill society in the United States, which led to the "free schools" movement in the 1960s and later the alternative schools movement. This reemergence of a more progressive educational philosophy was fueled by the civil rights and student protest movements.

This new generation of alternative educators expressed concern with a broader array of issues than those who had led the radical labor-versus-business movement of the 1920s. Themes of political and social emancipation—as well as economic—shaped the curriculum of this emerging free schools movement.[15] Inspired by the writings of John Holt, Herbert Kohl, Jonathan Kozol, Paulo Freire, and Allen Graubard, radical educators across the country founded "outside-the-system" free schools.[16]

These independent alternative, or free, schools were notable for their unstructured programs. Many eschewed grade levels or mandatory classes. Founded by groups of teachers and parents, they were run democratically. Teachers, parents, and students set educational standards, and made hiring decisions. These intimate familylike settings—in contrast to those at large, factorylike public schools—offered students a child-centered, or "humanistic," learning experience. By 1970 the New Schools Exchange, an information clearinghouse of free schools, listed more than 1,000 free schools nationwide. Almost all were private and independent.

The movement's leaders saw the public schools as authoritarian institutions that suppressed the natural curiosity and instincts of the young by placing too much emphasis on grades and discipline.[17] In response, they made certain that students enrolled in their schools were free to choose their subjects, follow their own interests, and learn at their own pace. A 1970 brochure for the Community School of Santa Barbara stated: "The idea is that freedom is a supreme good; that people, including young people, have a right to freedom, and that people who are free will in general be more open, more humane, more intelligent people. . . ."[18]

The child-centered educational themes that guided the educators at the free schools included:

1. The "personalization of education"—individual student needs and experiences are the starting point of all learning
2. Active learning—hands-on activities that involve the "whole" child are preferable to passive learning
3. Supportive teaching—the teacher is more an adviser than an authoritarian instructor
4. School as community—the school is a social community and education is a social activity
5. Community-based learning—students benefit from a variety of learning resources, especially those within the local community
6. Student participation—students take part in at least some of the major decision making at the school
7. Cooperation not competition—schools deemphasize competition for grades or class rank and stress cooperative forms of learning.[19]

Despite these shared philosophies, each of the alternative or free schools that arose in the 1960s and early 1970s was unique, reflecting the different styles and emphases of the educators who created and maintained them. Two surviving institutions illustrate this point. The Grassroots Free School in Tallahassee, Florida, founded in 1971, serves about 44 students ranging in age from 5 to 18. Students spend most of their day in the school yard, either working on self-directed projects or participating in small teacher-led discussion groups. When the ringing school bell signals the beginning of a new activity, they can elect to join in or continue working on their current project. "Those who want to go, go, and those who don't, don't," says director G. Patrick Seery, who calls this the "immersion method" of learning. At Grassroots, a student can devote an entire day or week to one project, because Seery and his teachers feel that any in-depth investigation will ultimately broaden to include several related areas and subjects.

At the Community School of Camden, Maine, founded in 1973, 16-to-20-year-old students who have dropped out of traditional high schools work and learn in a residential setting, in keeping with the school's mission: "To offer a highly experiential curriculum leading to a high school diploma, where students can discover a strong sense of self-worth while naming and addressing the issues which have sabotaged their success in school." While living at the school, students must hold a full-time job in Camden to help pay for their room and board and must also attend classes five evenings a week. Each student is assigned an adult mentor —a "one-to-one"—with whom he or she meets on a weekly basis. The range of classes offered at this independent, nonprofit school includes standard academic subjects as well as classes in parenting, substance abuse, conflict resolution, and self-esteem. Cooking, cleaning, and menu planning are also required courses, as students are expected to share in the daily responsibilities of running the school. They budget their own money, wash their own clothes, and clean their own rooms.

Other early free schools, now defunct, catered to a range of specific interests and needs. For instance, the Community School of Santa Barbara, located in a converted barracks on a hill, served 50 middle-class white students ages 3 to 14. The school included a wood and metal shop, and children worked outside to carve or weld sculpture as well as fix bikes and build toys. In contrast to this idyllic setting, the Children's Community Workshop School in New York City was situated in an economically and racially integrated neighborhood and had a diverse student enrollment—one-third white, one-third black, and one-third Puerto Rican. One of the central foci of the Children's Community Workshop was to create a multicultural, multilingual learning environment in which all students' backgrounds and experiences would be valued.

Although the design of the early free schools often varied, the central unifying aim was to create separate independent schools that offered students a viable alternative to what were considered authoritarian public schools. According to Mary Anne Raywid, one of the leading researchers on the history and impact of alternative education, "The repudiation of the dominant system probably marked the largest single area of agreement among the alternative educators of that first, 1960s, decade."[20]

Another unifying factor was the liberal attitudes of the alternative school educators. The free schools emphasized "freedom" for the individual student—not parental freedom to control their children's education, as espoused by the libertarians. In short, any "transgenerational dominance"—by teachers or parents— was rejected.

Most of the free schools also shared a commitment to charging little or no tuition, and were therefore often held together by "spit and string, and run mainly on the energy and excitement of people who have set out to do their own thing."[21]

This level of commitment and sense of mission is of course difficult to sustain; most of these independent free schools lasted only a few years—partly due to lack of funding, but also because of parents' fears that their children were not learning enough. According to data from the New Schools Exchange, the average life span of an independent alternative school in the early 1970s was about 18 months. Those that survived—at least 350 private alternative schools operate in the United States today—continue to exist on "spit and string" budgets and depend on teachers and parents for support.[22]

In 1970, at the peak of the free school movement, the desperate need for funds, coupled with a disdain for "authoritarian" public schools, led many alternative educators and parents to support the idea of government "tuition vouchers" for private or independent schools. At that time, the tuition voucher concept was being championed by Christopher Jencks, a liberal professor of sociology at Harvard University. In the spring of 1970, Jencks and his staff at the Cambridge-based Center for the Study of Public Policy completed a 250-page report on tuition vouchers for the federal Office of Economic Opportunity. Jencks then wrote an article for *The New Republic* in which he described in detail what he thought a fair, feasible voucher program should entail.[23]

Jencks called for government regulation of the plan to ensure that children of all races and socioeconomic backgrounds would have viable school choices. For instance, he suggested that students be admitted to the most popular schools of choice through a lottery system and that students from low-income families be given more tuition money—in the form of compensatory subsidies—than middle- and upper-class children.[24] Jencks's proposal also disallowed add-ons to vouchers, meaning that participating schools would not be able to charge more than the value of the vouchers for tuition.

Such a plan appealed to many members of the free school movement. Financially strapped, they saw their tax dollars flowing to purportedly unresponsive and authoritarian public schools. Government subsidies would help keep their schools alive, particularly the urban free schools that tried to attract children from low-income families.

But strong opposition from public school educators derailed the Jencks proposal, which produced only a small, undersubscribed federal demonstration project that led to one pseudo-voucher program (no private schools participated) in Alum Rock, California.[25]

Meanwhile, important changes were taking place within the public schools—and society in general—that sapped support from the political Left for tuition voucher plans. As a result of the civil rights movement, groups that had traditionally had little voice in the creation of public school policy—African-Americans, the handicapped, non-English speakers, and women—demanded greater access and a larger role in decision making. From the late 1960s until the late 1970s, public schools were compelled—by lawsuits as well as federal and state legislation—to respond to the needs of these formerly disfranchised groups.[26]

According to educational historian David Tyack, in an essay titled " 'Restructuring' in Historical Perspective," one way in which school districts responded to pressure from disaffected students was to expand the number of electives and create alternative schools—schools within schools and schools without walls. Such reforms provided greater choice for students and parents.[27]

Thus, by the early 1970s, school districts across the country had begun to borrow more liberal educational strategies from the independent free schools and to incorporate alternative schools and programs into their systems. Not only were public school districts becoming more open to alternative schools and programs, they were also gaining access to more federal money than ever before—money that was made available through War on Poverty legislation and was earmarked for specific or categorical reform efforts, including bilingual instruction, compensatory education, programs for the handicapped, ethnic-studies courses, and the creation of alternative schools.[28] The 1970 White House Conference on Children recommended "immediate, massive funding" for the development of alternative forms of public education. In 1972 the President's Commission on School Finance recommended that options in the form of alternative schools be provided to parents and students.[29] Between 1970 and 1975, the number of public alternative schools soared. In 1973 the International Consortium on Options in Public Education (ICOPE) first reported the growth of alternative schools in the United States, identifying 464 public alternative schools in 35 states. In 1975 ICOPE estimated the number to be as high as 5,000.[30]

This explosion and its impact on the educational options available to students was called "the only major movement in American education today" in a 1973 speech by Mario D. Fantini, one of the earliest chroniclers of the public alternative school movement.[31] In his well-known book *Public Schools of Choice*, Fantini argued that educators should respond to differences among students by diversifying the curriculum and organization of the public schools. Focusing squarely on student needs, he made little mention of parent entitlement to choice.[32]

In 1975 a survey of members of the National School Boards Association found that 25 percent of the respondents offered students educational options—either alternative programs within schools or separate alternative schools. The larger the district, the more likely it was to provide an alternative program. For instance, only 18 percent of districts with fewer than 600 students offered these programs, while 66 percent of those enrolling more than 25,000 students offered one or more alternative education options. The report detailing the results of the national survey concluded that "the alternative school concept is definitely not on the fringe of American public school activity: it is an important part of the program in many school districts and its significance is growing."[33]

Initially, many of these public alternative schools were, like the independent free schools before them, organized around the Summerhill philosophy and allowed students near-total autonomy. But, in time, new schools offered a wider variety of curricula and teaching methods better suited to the more structured public school framework.[34] For instance, state regulations mandate that public school students complete set required subjects.

Thus, while a public alternative school student can choose when and how he will learn science or math, he must, nevertheless, complete the required subjects.[35]

Despite the modifications of the free school curriculum, by the mid-1970s there was little doubt that the effort to incorporate alternative programs into what was seen as a rigid, highly bureaucratic public school system had shaken the foundation of education in America. Educators everywhere were shifting from a focus on efficiency and discipline toward a new emphasis on meeting the individual needs of students, much like their progressive predecessors of the 1930s. This time around, though, the movement toward child-centered education was decentralized. Vernon H. Smith, an alternative school researcher, wrote in 1974, "Because each alternative school has developed as a response to an individual community's educational concern rather than a response by the mainstream of the profession to a concern for the national interest, the alternatives represent the first evolutionary thrust in public education at the 'grass-roots' level."[36] As the popularity of public alternative schools continued to spread throughout the 1970s, programs were established at the insistence and with the input of students and parents. A 1974 survey of more than 300 public alternative schools by the National Alternative Schools Program (NASP) showed that these programs were indeed the result of grass-roots efforts. In 55 percent of the schools surveyed, teachers had provided the "major impetus" for the programs. And in almost all cases, students, parents, or community members also played decision-making roles.[37]

In a national survey of public school administrators by the National School Public Relations Association (NSPRA) in the late 1970s, 69 percent of the respondents said the main reason their districts had established alternative education programs was to "meet individual interests and needs." Another 23 percent gave similar but more specific responses, including "to meet the needs of a particular group of students, to motivate and interest students, to foster independence, and to match teaching and learning styles."[38] NSPRA found that public education agencies at all levels had modified regulations to facilitate development of alternative schools and programs. "Pluralism . . . is beginning to be acknowledged by an educational system whose institutional and conservative nature has not always recognized diversity as a virtue."[39]

THE PUBLIC ALTERNATIVES

Much like the private free schools that preceded them, the public alternative schools that came of age in the 1970s did not follow any set pattern. Created primarily to address the educational needs of specific groups of children, they were as distinct as their founders and the students who enrolled in them. Still, they shared a few common characteristics:

1. Nearly all were schools of choice, designed to provide educational options and attract students, parents, and teachers dissatisfied with the design or focus of traditional schools. Except for detention centers or continuation schools, which are often labeled "alternative schools" or alternative programs "of last resort" aimed at extremely troubled youth, most of the early public alternative schools were chosen by each student enrolled and by each staff member employed.

2. The schools provided educational programs distinctly different from those found in traditional schools—offering either a particular curricular emphasis, teaching method, school climate, or some combination. Hence, most alternative schools fit into one of the following categories:

> **Open Schools**, where learning activities are organized around interest centers within the classroom or building. Students are, for the most part, allowed to pursue their own interests and move from activity to activity. Instruction is much less

formal and more likely to be one-on-one as teachers guide students through individualized or small-group activities. More common at the elementary grade level, these frequently nongraded schools permit students to advance to more difficult material at their own pace.

Learning Centers or Theme Schools, which offer specialized curricula focused on particular disciplines or vocations, including math and science, the performing arts, and health careers.

Schools without Walls, in which students' primary learning activities take place within the community: in local businesses, museums, planetariums, nursing homes, etc. Required courses are taught by public school teachers, and a host of ancillary courses by community members, including librarians, curators, magazine editors, etc.[40]

Continuation Schools, which provide educational programs geared toward students who, for one reason or another, left their traditional school before graduating. These include dropout centers, reentry programs, pregnancy-maternity centers, evening and adult high schools, street academies, and the like.

Schools within Schools, where a smaller number of students and teachers create a separate learning program within a traditional school. The program can resemble those in any of the types mentioned above.[41]

3. The early alternative schools tended to be smaller than regular public schools. The 1974 NASP survey revealed that the vast majority had fewer than 200 students; only 12.6 percent had enrollments greater than 500.[42] Alternative school advocates argued that the smaller size was more conducive to student growth and learning.

4. When they began, public alternative schools typically had more comprehensive educational objectives that extended well beyond basic skills development or academic graduation requirements. Alternative educators were also concerned with raising

self-esteem, developing individual talent, encouraging appreciation of racial and cultural diversity, and preparing students for their various adult roles—consumer, voter, parent, spouse.[43] Hence, alternative schools tended to foster a cooperative rather than a competitive environment.

5. Successful alternative schools or programs sought relative autonomy from the public school bureaucracy which allowed them to be more innovative and responsive, encouraging feedback and evaluations from parents and students as they developed and modified their programs.[44]

6. Related to this receptivity, public alternative schools deliberately set out to encourage active participation—by the students, but also by the parents—in the schools' culture and ethos. In addition, the schools tended to be far more responsive than conventional public schools to needs within their communities.[45]

These basic characteristics distinguished the hundreds of public alternative schools founded in the 1970s from their traditional counterparts. They reflect the fundamental educational goals that were driving the alternative school educators. Clearly, the central motivating force behind these schools was to make education responsive to a student's individual needs and talents. Because this philosophy underscored the notion that there was no single school model that could achieve that end, student choice was important.

To the extent that alternative school educators also tried to involve parents and community members, teach children to understand and appreciate diversity, and make schools responsive to the needs of the community, their second, underlying goal was obviously to serve the common good. But because these early alternatives were public schools *and* schools of choice, a critical "common good" question arose: To what extent were all students equally well served by the proliferation of public alternative schools?

In the current school choice debate, both advocates and opponents of choice argue more about who will have access to the "good" schools of choice than what these schools will actually look like. But the 1970s thrust toward developing more educational options within the public system resulted, in most instances, in enough alternative programs to meet all students' demands. The following description of the creation and expansion of an alternative school in Berkeley, California, from a 1973 article by Joan Chesler, shows how districts met the growing demands for educational options during this era:

> Berkeley Community High is an alternative or mini-high school now in its fourth year of functioning. It is the first of a series of alternative high schools within the Berkeley school system and has served as a working model for the development of two more alternative schools within Berkeley High.
>
> Community High began with 100 students as an outgrowth of a summer drama program developed by a group of Berkeley (High School) staff members. Teachers developed this experience into a full-time school program, and it began in 1968 as a school-within-a-school. Since they wanted to give students meaningful responsibility and control, teachers worked actively with the student body to generate a new program and attempted to develop a student-oriented curriculum providing a good deal of freedom for individual work. Pressure from other local students and parents served as an impetus for the creation of two additional alternative schools in February 1971. . . . At the same time, Community High divided into small tribal units as a response to its increased size. In 1971 there were 300 students in the program. One of the tribes, Black House, split off from Community High, becoming responsible to the school district administration rather than to Berkeley High's principal. Black House recently opened admissions to all black students in the larger Berkeley High School.[46]

Although Community High and its satellite "tribes" were forced to deal with the issue of how multiracial each tribe should be, overall student "access" to an alternative program of his or her choice was not an issue. Even though escalating costs and shrinking tax revenues were forcing cutbacks in programs and services in school districts across the country during this period, school boards continued to support expansion of alternative schools in response to student and parent demand.[47]

The number of alternative schools known as continuation schools and geared toward the academic and emotional needs of high school dropouts, delinquents, or teen mothers grew considerably during this period. Educators in traditional schools rarely opposed the creation of so-called continuation schools because these programs siphoned off students who required extra counseling and services, allowing the traditional schools to focus on less troubled, academically successful students.

For those popular alternative schools that could not be duplicated or expanded to meet student demand, lottery systems were frequently used to select applicants. Equity and access issues were of less concern in the 1970s than they are now for popular magnet schools, largely because these early alternative schools were not designed to compete for recognition as the "best" schools with the "best" students; they were grass-roots organizations aimed at nurturing the students who chose a particular curriculum or approach to learning.[48] They were not elitist institutions designed to attract students with the highest standardized test scores or GPAs, unlike the "exam schools" that preceded them—e.g., Boston Latin and Bronx Science. Student choice worked in the 1970s because the financial and political support for public alternative schools was strong enough to ensure an adequate range of options to meet the demand from a diverse student population. This would not be the case when the back-to-basics reforms of the 1980s took hold.

While little recent research on alternative schools has been conducted, some of the data collected in the early 1980s, as well as current anecdotal information from individual schools and districts, suggests that alternative schools in the public sector continue to provide thousands of families with significant educational choices they would not otherwise have. At the same time, some evidence suggests that hundreds of public alternative schools were standardized during the 1980s to the point where they were far less effective at meeting the needs of individual students.

With the passing of the "rights revolution" of the 1960s and 1970s, and the emergence of a more conservative national mood, the push for more alternative forms of education fizzled. Education in the 1980s meant less emphasis on the needs and talents of individuals and greater focus on a unidimensional pursuit of "excellence" as narrowly measured by standardized tests. According to Thomas Toch in his book *In the Name of Excellence*:

> The conservative education agenda—which was also championed in the late 1970s by think tanks such as the Heritage Foundation and the Ethics and Public Policy Center, by Republican members of Congress . . . and editorially by *Fortune* magazine and *The Wall Street Journal*—was in turn part of a wide-ranging conservative intellectual and political assault on the liberal values and social policies of the 1960s and 1970s that landed Ronald Reagan in the White House.[49]

The "conservative education agenda" emphasized high standards, high test scores, a return to the basic core subjects, and a sink-or-swim attitude toward individual achievement. It was a backlash against earlier efforts to encourage "the fullest possible participation of all students in the nation's educational system."[50] According to Chester E. Finn, an assistant secretary of education in the Reagan administration and perhaps the most vocal proponent of the "excellence movement," liberal policymakers possessed "a near-boundless confidence in the ability of the national government to deploy its resources in ways that reduce the educational consequences of individual differences." This devotion, Finn charged, had led the "liberal consensus" to define school success in terms of opportunities and resources provided to students rather than academic achievement.[51]

In order to measure excellence in terms of academic achievement, the leaders of the so-called excellence movement needed an easy and concise gauge of student learning. In 1984 the Department of Education, under the leadership of former secretary T. H. Bell, began ranking the states' performances largely on the basis of the standardized college admissions test results. This practice, which received wide publicity and focused the nation on standardized test scores, was continued by Bell's successors.[52]

In this new political climate, alternative education in its most radical form soon became a relic of a bygone era. Many schools without walls and open schools were shut down or standardized to look more traditional.[53]

Meanwhile, a new category of alternative schools—known as "fundamental" or "academics-plus" schools—emerged. With their back-to-basics curriculum emphasis on preparing students for standardized tests and teacher-directed instruction, they were the conservative counterparts to the more progressive programs of the alternative education movement, and they constituted the fastest-growing option in alternative education in the late 1970s and 1980s. One of the first and best-known examples of an academics-plus alternative school was the John Marshall Fundamental School in Pasadena, California, which began as a K-12 school in 1973 and then split into separate elementary and secondary schools in 1975. To clearly distinguish itself from other alternative schools of the time, John Marshall required extra homework, gave letter grades, established a dress code, enforced strict discipline, and employed rigid ability grouping or tracking based on standardized tests.[54]

Even before these more conservative alternative schools began sprouting up around the country, signs of another powerful "school choice" movement appeared. By the mid-1970s, federal courts overseeing school desegregation cases began allowing school districts to use magnet or specialty schools as part of their court-ordered remedies. Because magnets are schools of choice that, by definition, offer a distinct curriculum or instructional approach in order to attract students of different races, they can be remarkably similar to public alternative schools. In fact, many alternative schools were turned into magnet schools—a change that was largely symbolic, since alternative schools were often the most integrated schools in their districts. After Congress passed the Magnet Schools Assistance Act in 1984, making federal grant money available to districts that were using magnet schools to desegregate, the shift toward calling public schools of choice magnet schools instead of alternative schools accelerated. To this day, the two labels are frequently used interchangeably.[55]

As many of the popular alternative schools were converted into magnet schools and the more radical alternatives became casualties of a conservative era, a larger percentage of the public schools that maintained their "alternative school" identity provided continuation programs for dropouts and teen mothers. The most recent national data for secondary schools indicate that almost two-thirds of public alternative schools serve potential and actual dropouts.[56] A 1988 Washington State survey revealed that 35 percent of the state's 104 public alternative schools were continuation schools, and another 12 percent were fundamental or academics-plus schools. Only 2 percent were schools without walls and only 1 percent were open schools.[57]

Such data suggest a dramatic shift in emphasis and focus for alternative education since the mid-1970s, when a nationwide survey revealed that only 20 percent of all public alternatives were continuation schools, 15 percent were open schools, and 6 percent were schools without walls (no data were available on fundamental alternative schools).[58]

The growth of continuation programs—often called "soft jails" or schools of last resort—raised serious questions about the role and purpose of public alternative schools and contributed to a public perception of "alternative education" as appropriate chiefly for students who were academic failures. This lowered the demand for alternative programs among students who were surviving, if not excelling, in their regular schools.

Today the renewed political commitment to "school choice" has revitalized interest in alternative education—both public and private. Although the current political thrust toward greater parental choice of schools has a different, more conservative tone than that of the movement that gave birth to radical forms of alternative education in the 1960s and 1970s, the triumphs and perils of alternative education can and should inform future educational policy decisions. Furthermore, those who take up the call for private-school choice plans and tuition vouchers as the answer to the unresponsive public education "monopoly" should realize that the conservative-led educational reforms of the 1980s squelched many of the public alternative schools—schools that had provided meaningful educational choices to parents and students for many years.

SUCCESS AND FAILURE OF ALTERNATIVE SCHOOLS

Perhaps it is just one of the many ironies of educational policy-making in the last decade that a political drive known as the "excellence movement" would severely curtail an existing educational effort that had proved successful at increasing educational achievement.

Overall, the research on alternative education, much of which was conducted in the late 1970s and focuses on the effects of alternative schools on student achievement and emotional development and teacher efficacy, points to quite favorable results. It is, however, difficult to generalize about the educational impact of alternative schools because each is unique.

STUDENTS

Alternative schools often compare favorably with conventional schools in measures of academic achievement and usually surpass them in the affective area. For instance, Mary Anne Raywid's review of the research on public schools of choice concluded that in terms of standardized achievement measures—e.g., test scores and college admissions—graduates of alternative schools performed as well as or better than their counterparts in traditional schools.[59] An early report on public alternative education summarized the findings of several evaluation studies of elementary and secondary public alternative schools and concluded that, in most cases, the academic achievement of students either improved or remained stable. In almost all cases, however, the alternative schools were successful in the affective realm (i.e., attitudes and attendance).[60] But this report also found that alternative schools had difficulty sustaining student interest in school governance and decision making, and that students and staff members often had a difficult time balancing personal responsibility and increased personal freedom.[61]

In 1981 Gerald Smith, Thomas Gregory, and Richard Pugh studied seven alternative and six traditional high schools and measured students' and teachers' need for security, feelings of belonging, esteem, and self-actualization. Students and teachers in the alternative schools scored significantly higher than their traditional school counterparts in the areas of esteem, self-actualization, and "belonging," which meant their school provided an environment that emphasized social relationships and belonging to a group. Their "need for security"—i.e., insecurity or the opposite of being self-assured—was lower, although not significantly so.[62]

Reviewing several studies on alternative schools conducted in the 1980s, Timothy Young found evidence that students enrolled in alternative schools have more positive attitudes about themselves and their schools than similar students attending conventional schools. He also found that when students transfer into alternative schools their absentee rates decline and their in-school behavior improves. Furthermore, alternative school students report more personal contacts with teachers and classmates; one study revealed that alternative school teachers are more likely to praise and acknowledge students.[63]

Vernon Smith, Daniel J. Burke, and Robert D. Barr suggest, based on their examination of alternative schools, that there is another beneficial side effect, which they call the "psychology of choice." They state that students and parents are more loyal to a school they have chosen than to one chosen for them. In addition, they cite what they call a "therapy of involvement" associated with alternative schools: "When parents, students, teachers, and administrators are involved in planning the program, they establish a healthy interaction which creates a spirit of cooperation hard to duplicate in other ways."[64]

TEACHERS

The smaller body of research on educators suggests that teaching in an alternative school can be a rewarding but overwhelming experience. For instance, in the Educational Research Service (ERS) review of 27 public alternative schools, evaluators often noted a high degree of teacher dedication to program goals and success. But they also found teachers in alternative schools had exhaustive work schedules and experienced heavier-than-usual emotional demands and that teacher turnover was in some cases very high.[65]

A 1982 survey of 1,200 public alternative programs by the Project on Alternative Education (PAE)—the largest survey to date on alternative programs—found that staff morale is extremely high in alternative schools. Of the responding staff members, 90 percent expressed a sense of ownership of their programs, and 90 percent were willing to take on even more professional activities and obligations, especially networking with staff members from other alternative schools.[66]

MODEL ALTERNATIVES

In a 1983 *Phi Delta Kappan* article summarizing the PAE survey, Mary Anne Raywid listed what she saw as the four main factors that contribute to alternative school success.

First, small size is a crucial factor in developing and maintaining educational programs tailored to the needs, free will, and talents of each individual child.

Second, choice on the part of students, parents, and teachers is essential. "There are grounds for speculating that choice may be even more important for teachers than for students," Raywid wrote, citing greater improvements in teachers' attendance rates in chosen alternative schools.

Third, extended roles for students and staff are necessary. Because everyone in an alternative school has a larger domain of responsibility and discretion than in conventional schools, children and adults interact in several different contexts, and the schools take on a much larger mission than that of simply instilling information.

Fourth, relative autonomy from the rules and regulations that leave most educators feeling powerless is critical. As Raywid noted, "Somehow alternative schools manage to achieve enough independence to let staff members design and carry out their own vision of schooling." Alternative school educators report high levels of control over decisions essential to a school's operation. This "power" is shared among the staff to the degree that, in many alternative schools, teachers play an important part in hiring staff and allocating funds. In the most autonomous situations, students also share in decision making.[67]

Raywid's research emphasizes that the benefits of school choice can be reaped within the public system when alternative school educators are given greater autonomy to "carry out their visions." Unfortunately, this does not always happen. Teachers are often constrained in what and how they teach by federal, state, and district-level mandates and competency tests. School administrators also feel trapped by federal and state regulations, union contracts and negotiations, etc. But for alternative schools to thrive and provide real choices to students and parents, they must maintain a great deal of autonomy over program planning, curriculum content, and instructional methods.[68]

All four of the success factors that Raywid discusses are in place in New York City's Community School District No. 4, which encompasses much of East Harlem and offers perhaps the most highly touted school choice program in the country. In 1974, teachers and administrators in this poor and predominantly Hispanic school district offered parents and students three small alternative schools: a junior high for students with a history of behavioral problems, a junior high that specialized in the performing arts, and a progressive elementary school guided by Deweyan philosophy.[69]

Each year thereafter, the district launched several new alternative junior high programs within existing schools. By 1982, every junior high school building in the district consisted of four or more alternative schools of choice. Thus, "zoned" or "neighborhood" junior high schools no longer exist in East Harlem. Every sixth-grader who lives in District 4 can now choose which of the 23 alternative school programs he or she will enroll in the following year.

At the elementary level, neighborhood schools remain the norm in District 4, except for five alternative schools, three of which are based on Deweyan philosophy, two bilingual. At the high school level, students in New York apply to one or more of the city's 200 public highs, which operate on a citywide basis, although one of District 4's junior high schools, Central Park East Secondary School, now includes grades 9 through 12.[70]

Each of the 23 alternative junior high schools is about one-fifth the size of the four junior high schools it replaced. (While a typical junior high school in New York City may easily have 1,200 to 1,400 students, enrollment at alternative schools rarely exceeds 250.) Each of the four junior high school buildings is managed by one principal, but the alternative school programs are led by a teacher who serves as a director and oversees all the curricular and instructional planning.

Most of the alternative schools in District 4 are designed around curricular themes—biomedical studies, communication arts, performing arts, marine biology, etc.—but also reflect a particular style of pedagogy adopted by their founders. In addition, these schools are staffed by educators who have, in almost all cases, chosen to teach in them.

According to Deborah Meier, one of District 4's most respected educators and principal of the Central Park East Secondary School, the early alternative schools in the now-famous district were "rarely the result of a central plan from the district office, but rather tended to be the brainchildren of particular individuals or groups of teachers. They were initiated by the people who planned to teach in them."[71] Seymour Fliegel, former director of District 4's alternative programs, recalled that "in East Harlem, we extended the concept of choice to teachers as well as parents and gave our educators the freedom and support they needed to see their educational dreams become a reality."[72]

For sixth-graders in District 4, the school choice process begins in February, when each student receives a copy of a booklet describing the alternative junior high schools. Orientation sessions for parents and students are held where the directors of the various alternative schools discuss programs and answer questions. During March and April, sixth-graders and their parents are encouraged to visit the alternative schools, and in May each student submits an application with six school choices. According to John Falco, the assistant superintendent in District 4 responsible for the school choice process, 97 percent of the sixth-graders are "admitted" to one of their top three junior highs of choice.

Admission to District 4's junior high schools does not entail a highly stressful and competitive process based on narrow criteria such as test scores and GPAs. Like the public alternative school movement that came before them, District 4 alternative schools focus on meeting the needs of students. Because the choice plan operates within the public school system and the district is responsible for the education of all resident students, there is a place for everyone.

To ensure that all students have viable choices, District 4 administrators monitor the popularity of the various alternative schools. Less popular schools are closed or they are restructured to make them more desirable. This minimizes the chances that students will be forced to enroll in undesirable schools. Still, some District 4 schools are more popular than others, and there has yet to be a comprehensive evaluation of which students stand the greatest chance of being admitted to the most coveted slots and which end up with their second or third choice.

But because District 4 serves a 60 percent Hispanic and 39

percent African-American resident student population, and about 80 percent of the district's 14,000 students qualify for free or reduced-price lunches, access and equity issues between white and nonwhite or poor and nonpoor students are minimized. In fact, ten of District 4's alternative schools have received federal school desegregation funds under the Magnet Schools Assistance Act and have desegregated by drawing white students from outside district boundaries. Thus, District 4, a predominantly poor and minority district, now has some of New York City's most integrated and sought-after schools—schools where children from East Harlem have first choice.

The District 4 choice plan contains the necessary ingredients for success—small schools, guaranteed student and teacher choice, an expanded role for both students and parents, and a great deal of teacher and school autonomy to create and implement the programs.

The only measures of District 4's success yet available are standardized test scores and student admissions to the city's examination schools. In 1973 only ten students from District 4 were admitted to New York's highly competitive examination schools—Bronx Science, Stuyvesant, Brooklyn Technical, and LaGuardia. Since the mid-1980s, East Harlem has sent more than 300 eighth-graders to these schools each year.[73] In terms of test scores, 17 years ago District 4 was ranked 32nd out of 32 community school districts on standardized reading and math tests. At that time, only 15 percent of the students read at or above grade level. By the early 1980s more than 50 percent of District 4 students were reading at or above grade level, and in 1981 the East Harlem district ranked 15th among the city's 32 districts in reading and 21st in math. According to a recent report on school choice by the Carnegie Foundation for the Advancement of Teaching, however, District 4's reading test scores have dropped off dramatically in the last five years. By 1992, only 38 percent of the students scored at or above grade level on reading tests, and East Harlem now ranks 22nd out of 32 districts in reading.[74]

Despite the less than clear-cut relationship between school choice and student achievement, advocates of tuition-voucher, private-school choice plans continue to use District 4 as an example of how parental choice works in education. But the District 4 choice plan is a far cry from a voucher plan in which the educational fate of the children would be determined in the marketplace instead of in a government-run school district responsible for assuring that all students receive a minimally adequate education. What District 4 illustrates is that school choice programs can work within the public sector without draining off precious public education funds into private religious and elite schools.

LESS TRIUMPHANT TALES

While District 4 in New York was dazzling educators and the national media, and being hailed by commentators on both the political Left and Right as evidence that "school choice" works, other public alternative schools across the country were struggling to survive and losing public support and interest. Hundreds of once-thriving public alternative schools of choice were minimized and marginalized by the educational politics of the 1980s.

Everything that was wrong with America—especially the economy—was blamed on the public schools, as it had been in the late 1950s after the Soviets launched *Sputnik*. According to the critics, college-entrance test scores were down (although the pool of test takers was also changing to include low-income students who in the past had not continued through high school), high school students were taking too many "soft" courses and not enough of the basics—math, science, English, and history —and schools were too focused on the nonacademic needs of students.[75]

As noted earlier, the response by many state departments of education and local school districts to these criticisms and the politically powerful "excellence movement" in general was to increase graduation requirements, decrease the number of elective courses offered, and place greater emphasis on test taking and test results.[76]

These back-to-basics reforms, strongly advocated by President Reagan's second Secretary of Education, William J. Bennett, and his assistant, Chester E. Finn, resulted in far less student and parental choice in public education. Public alternative schools, once the source of a wide range of curricular and instructional options in public education, lost much of their political and financial support in an era when schools were told that "more of the same" would solve the country's deep-seated educational and economic problems.

At the same time, increased bureaucratic constraints on educators, resulting from the growing number of state-mandated requirements, further limited opportunities for grass-roots innovations at the school level.

President Bush and his Education Secretary, Lamar Alexander, carried the Reagan-era "conformity reforms" one step further by calling for a set of national standards for each of five core subjects and national tests to measure student comprehension of these national standards. President Clinton and his Education Secretary, Richard W. Riley, appear headed in the same direction in terms of national standards.

The impact on alternative schools of the "excellence movement" and the efforts to create national standards has been devastating. In cities across the country, public alternative schools have had to struggle not only against local bureaucracies and union rules that come close to strangling their innovations, but also against a hostile political culture. Educational policymakers, from the U.S. Department of Education to the local school boards, are advocating that principals, teachers, students, and parents conform to rules, regulations, and standards that have been set at the federal, state, and district level. For example, in May 1992, the Denver Public Schools' administration announced plans to close the city's only alternative school, High School Redirection. The reasons given for the closing were "budget constraints and opposition to innovations embraced by the school."[77] In other words, the alternative school's philosophy and approach were not in line with the national policy agenda.

High School Redirection opened in 1988 to serve Denver students who were seen as potential dropouts. Instead of assigning letter grades, Redirection teachers evaluated academic progress through student projects, essays, and personal journals. Students were allowed to work at their own pace, meeting with their teachers for weekly counseling sessions. Many of the 1992 Redirection graduates said that if it weren't for this program, they would not have completed high school.

Parents and students protested the closing, but to no avail. The school district's director of alternative education, Emilio Esquibel, was quoted in *The New York Times* as saying, "The school district wanted to see traditional types of things, like grades. . . . We [district officials] just weren't willing to guarantee these students who were educated at High School Redirection a diploma. That was the bottom line."[78]

The New Orleans Free School was founded in the late 1960s as a private alternative school. Due to lack of funds, it joined the New Orleans Public School system in 1973. Since the merger, the school has been forced to increase enrollment from 37 to 300 students, switch locations three times, hire teachers and staff who do not necessarily agree with the school's philosophy, and face frequent threats from the school board that it will close the school down.

"I'm a strong and vocal critic of bureaucratizing education and a strong and vocal advocate of choice and more school site autonomy," said principal Robert M. Ferris in an interview.

Although Ferris has managed to maintain much of the uniqueness of the New Orleans Free School as an inquiry-based, experiential, and creative program, he noted that it is an uphill battle at a time when policymakers emphasize "right" answers, rigidity, routine, and reproducing knowledge.

In an article published in a 1991 newsletter of the National Coalition of Alternative Community Schools, Ferris wrote:

> The emphasis all too often is not on the joy, excitement and/or challenge of learning; rather it is on skill development, mastery

of isolated skills, sequence of skills, test taking skills, etc. Curricula are no longer based on interests, needs or curiosity but are dominated by what is on the tests.[79]

The end result is that too many of the public alternative schools that have managed to survive have either compromised their goals and missions or, as mentioned earlier, maintained the thankless role of being schools of last resort.

ALTERNATIVE SCHOOLS AND THE CURRENT PUSH FOR SCHOOL CHOICE

As policymakers and voters debate the future scope and direction of school choice policy in the United States, they must keep in mind that hundreds of public educational systems, especially those in urban areas, have been providing families with viable school choices for more than 20 years.

Although the alternative schools movement of the 1970s was curtailed by the conservative reforms of the 1980s, successful alternative programs demonstrate that public school educators can respond to the needs of the children they serve. More important, these educators are able and willing to meet the individual educational needs of their "clients" even in the absence of competition from private schools or other school districts for their public education dollars.

Another important lesson to be learned from the history of alternative schools is that the best schools of choice are created by educators who will work in them—not by a national "excellence" mandate, a slew of standardized tests, or a competitive voucher plan. Instead, educators help to forge the shape and scope of promising schools of choice from the needs and interests of the children they will serve. This basic philosophical principle, a carryover from the free schools movement that inspired the growth of public alternative education, remains critically important.

In short, school choice advocates who wish to infuse competitive, free-market principles into public education miss the exact reason why public alternative schools of choice have succeeded. But public-school choice programs can go one step further. As the next chapter demonstrates, parental choice in education can be designed and implemented in such a way that it simultaneously serves the individual needs of children *and* the larger, common good of our society.

CHAPTER THREE

SCHOOL DESEGREGATION BY CHOICE

FROM FREEDOM OF CHOICE PLANS

TO CONTROLLED CHOICE

Although Americans tend to associate desegregation with protests and mandatory busing plans, few people realize that thousands of children are participating in a desegregation plan by attending the public school of their choice. School choice has figured continuously, and sometimes controversially, in the history of school desegregation since 1954, the year in which the Supreme Court ruled in *Brown v. Board of Education* that the doctrine of "separate but equal" had no place in public education. For more than three decades, actions intended to protect the rights of parents to choose their child's school have intersected—and often conflicted—with efforts to provide African-American and Latino students with access to a quality education. It is no wonder, then, that desegregation efforts incorporating some degree of parental choice have been received as a welcome compromise between the rights of individuals and the needs of the society.

Few Americans would disagree that the common good is better served when educational policy-making is guided by certain "nonneutral" principles, including equal educational opportunity, a commitment to diversity and tolerance, and a guarantee of freedom of association for people of all races. To the extent that school choice is a means of achieving these educational ends, it should be supported. But not all voluntary, or choice-oriented, desegregation plans succeed at spreading educational opportunity; some limit it to a handful of students and schools, leaving other schools more segregated and unequal than before.

This chapter examines different school desegregation policies that incorporate parent and student choice and explains why some serve the common good better than others.

FREEDOM OF CHOICE PLANS

In the ten years following the *Brown* decision, school districts throughout the South instituted "freedom of choice" plans—nominal desegregation plans that allowed black students to choose formerly all-white schools and white students to choose formerly all-black schools. Rather than dismantling the dual system of separate black and white schools, these freedom of choice plans were used by southern school districts to forestall any meaningful school desegregation efforts.

According to Gary Orfield, a Harvard professor and expert on school desegregation policy, in the 1960s hundreds of southern school districts operated "freedom of choice" plans in which a small percentage of black students transferred schools, but almost no whites did, even though many of the black schools were often closer to white students' homes and offered distinctive educational programs.[1] Freedom of choice plans failed to desegregate southern schools because they placed the entire burden of dismantling the 200-year-old system of racial segregation on black students and their parents. White school officials in charge of enrollments were able to easily block the transfer of black students into formerly white schools. Coercion and intimidation on the part of white educators, parents, and students dissuaded many African-Americans from even applying for transfers to white schools.

The barriers to desegregation that black students faced under these choice plans were brought to the attention of the Supreme Court in 1968. The case, *Green v. County School Board of New Kent County*, involved a small rural community of about 4,500 in eastern Virginia. In New Kent, as in many rural areas throughout the South, there was little residential segregation; blacks and whites had lived side by side for hundreds of years.

The county had only two schools: the George W. Watkins school in the western portion, which enrolled the district's 740 black students, and the New Kent school in the east, which enrolled the district's 550 white students. Each of these schools combined the elementary and secondary grades to serve students from kindergarten through 12th grade. The district used 21 school buses on a daily basis—11 serving the Watkins school and 10 serving the New Kent school. As was typical in the South at that time, these buses traveled overlapping routes in order to bring black and white students from the same neighborhoods to different schools.[2]

In 1964 Virginia enacted the Pupil Placement Act, which basically stripped the local school districts of their authority to assign children to a particular school. Under the act, students were automatically reassigned to the schools they had attended the previous year unless they submitted an application to the state board of education and a transfer was approved. Students seeking enrollment in public schools for the first time were assigned to schools at the discretion of the state board. Christine Rossell, who has written extensively on voluntary or choice-oriented desegregation, found that this type of pupil placement law was not unusual in the South during the early 1960s. In states that had passed such laws, students were assigned to racially segregated schools according to race, and requests for transfers were considered on an individual basis, in light of various "nonracial" factors. As Rossell explains, "These included the 'psychological effect' on the student, the 'psychological qualifications' of the student for the curriculum at the requested school, the possibility of disruptions within the school, and the possibility of protest or economic retaliation by whites against blacks in the community."[3]

A host of other arguments were also used to deny transfers. According to a 1962 report by the U.S. Commission on Civil

Rights, what was happening in southern states with pupil-placement legislation—and in districts like New Kent—was that the state placement boards, in an effort to minimize desegregation efforts, were employing three criteria to keep black students out of white schools. The boards required that student transfers not upset: (1) the orderly administration of the public schools, (2) the competent instruction of the pupils enrolled, or (3) the health, safety, education, and general welfare of the pupils.[4] School districts or the state pupil-placement board, therefore, could easily make a case that a requested student transfer from an all-black to an all-white school would create an unnecessary hardship on the district or the student community, based on one of these three criteria.

Under Virginia's Pupil Placement Act, the schools throughout the state remained segregated, in part because of the state board's intent to maintain separate black and white schools and in part because few blacks applied for transfers they did not think they could obtain. During the first year of Virginia's Pupil Placement Act, none of the black students in New Kent County applied for a transfer to the New Kent school under this statute and no white student applied for admission to the Watkins school.[5]

But also in 1964 the U.S. Congress passed the Civil Rights Act, which withheld federal funds from institutions that excluded any person on the basis of race, color, or national origin. In order to remain eligible for federal funds, the local school boards in Virginia and other southern states adopted "freedom of choice" plans, which they said would provide African-American students greater access to white schools and thereby lead to desegregation. The New Kent County freedom of choice plan, enacted in 1965, required first- and eighth-grade students to select one of the two schools in the district. Students in other grades could apply for a school transfer; otherwise they would be automatically reassigned to the school they had previously attended. In New Kent County, as elsewhere in the South where freedom of choice plans were in place, student choices could technically be denied only on the grounds of overcrowding. But a 1965 report by the Student

Non-Violent Coordinating Committee explains why the number of black students who attended desegregated schools under freedom of choice plans was so small:

> The method is simple . . . get a few Negroes to sign up to attend white schools, and then let the local citizens "encourage" them to withdraw their applications. An even better way is to reject all Negro applicants because of overcrowding, bad character, improper registration, or any other excuses. . . .[6]

As a result of harassment by local whites and the tactics employed by state pupil-placement boards, by 1965 almost 94 percent of southern black students remained in all-black schools, and in several states only the slightest change had been made in the system of separate and unequal schools. In New Kent County, by 1967 none of the white students had opted to transfer to the all-black Watkins school, but 115 black students (up from 35 in 1965 and 111 in 1966) had been allowed to transfer to the New Kent school. Nevertheless, 85 percent of the district's black students remained in the segregated school.[7]

In the late 1960s, the federal Department of Education's Office for Civil Rights (OCR) and the U.S. Justice Department tried to tighten federal guidelines for freedom of choice plans. First, they identified 25 "problem areas" in the guidelines of the choice plans, including the method of distribution of school choice forms to black parents. In most districts, forms were given to students to take home and were collected from the students or parents by school principals. Many black parents were afraid to present their principal with a form indicating that they no longer wanted their child in his or her school. With no guarantee that their transfer request would be accepted, the possibility of alienating the local principal was frightening.[8] In response to such findings, OCR created a new requirement that school choice forms must be mailed to parents and that parents must also be permitted to return the forms to the district office by mail. Other guidelines, such as the intimidating wording of the letter to black parents and the length of time parents were given to respond, were adjusted to make school choice more feasible for black students.[9] Still, other methods of intimidation at the school and community level remained in place, and local districts and state pupil-placement boards continued to control the decision-making process for the so-called school choice plans. Little desegregation occurred.[10]

Several months before the New Kent County freedom of choice plan went into effect, a group of black plaintiffs sued the state and the school district on grounds of discrimination. In 1966 the federal district court ruled in favor of the state and approved New Kent's freedom of choice plan as an adequate step toward dismantling the dual school system. The U.S. Court of Appeals for the Fourth Circuit upheld the lower court's ruling.

In 1968 the Supreme Court reversed the lower courts' decisions in the *Green* case and dramatically changed the meaning and implications of "school desegregation" and "freedom of choice" plans in the South. Writing the majority opinion, Justice William J. Brennan, Jr., reviewed the New Kent School Board's position:

> . . . it had fully discharged its obligation to abolish the dual system of education by adopting a plan by which every student, regardless of race, may "freely" choose the school he will attend. The Board attempts to cast the issue in its broadest form by arguing that its "freedom-of-choice" plan may be faulted only by reading the Fourteenth Amendment as universally requiring "compulsory integration."[11]

Despite the school board's arguments, the Supreme Court ruled that New Kent's "freedom of choice" plan was not sufficient to achieve a "racially nondiscriminatory school system" and convert the district into a system "without a 'white' school and a 'Negro' school, but just schools." The ruling stated that the choice plan had operated simply to burden children and their parents with a responsibility that the Court had placed squarely on the school board.[12]

Without ordering a specific desegregation program for the school board, the Court stated that "the burden on a school board today is to come forward with a plan that promises realistically to work, and promises to realistically work now."[13]

The *Green* decision marked an important turning point in the history of American educational policy and the long-held belief in local control. The Supreme Court ruling was interpreted to mean that southern school districts must do more than provide the means by which students could desegregate themselves, so to speak, by choosing a school. Districts were now required to ensure that desegregation actually took place. While *Green* did not rule out the possibility of districts offering parents and students a genuine choice about which desegregated schools they would attend, the decision, along with the Court's 1971 ruling in *Swann v. Charlotte-Mecklenburg Board of Education*, led to a substantial increase in mandatory student reassignment plans —commonly known as "forced busing"—and a significant decrease in the degree of "choice" that either black or white parents had as to where their children would go to school. In fact, it was the *Swann* decision that sanctioned district courts to require "involuntary" means of achieving truly nondiscriminatory student assignments.

Unlike the *Green* case, which involved a small rural town with only two schools and a great deal of residential integration, the *Swann* case concerned the desegregation of a large metropolitan area—Charlotte, North Carolina, and surrounding Mecklenburg County. The Charlotte-Mecklenburg school district enrolled more than 84,000 students in 107 schools. Most of the 24,000 black students in the district lived within the city of Charlotte, and close to two-thirds of these were enrolled in 21 inner-city schools. Housing segregation, therefore, was an important issue in the case, as was the argument that the school district had perpetuated racial isolation by constructing new schools in racially segregated neighborhoods while closing existing schools in neighborhoods that appeared likely to become racially mixed because of changing residential patterns.[14]

The central issue in *Swann* was whether or not the courts could require the school system to use racial quotas, newly drawn attendance zones, and transportation (busing) to correct racial segregation in the district. In other words, could the courts integrate the schools against the wishes of parents who had chosen to live near particular neighborhood schools? Given that the Charlotte-Mecklenburg school district had, for several decades before the *Brown* decision, assigned students to racially segregated schools without giving parents any choice, a ruling in favor of mandatory desegregation was not theoretically different from state-enforced segregation. In both cases, there is little regard for personal freedom and individual choice.

The main distinction, of course, was that few whites objected to mandatory segregation, but many opposed mandatory desegregation. Whites in the South had been told for decades that segregated black schools were grossly inferior to segregated white schools. After all, this was the stated legal reason why civil rights leaders demanded school desegregation.[15] Moreover, widespread racist attitudes that painted blacks as genetically or culturally inferior also made some white parents resistant to school desegregation plans.

But the Supreme Court, impatient with the pace of integration in southern school districts, ruled in *Swann* that while "the constitutional command to desegregate schools does not mean that every school in every community must always reflect the racial composition of the school system as a whole . . . the very limited use made of mathematical ratios was within the equitable remedial discretion of the District Court." The Court also found that "affirmative action" through altered attendance zones—or student assignments—is proper to achieve a truly nondiscriminatory system. This meant that a school district could be ordered to "pair" a black elementary and a white elementary school, sending all the kindergarten-through-second-grade students from both schools to one building and assigning all the third-through-sixth-graders to the other building. Furthermore, the Court ruled that local school authorities may be required to use bus transportation as a tool to desegregate. "Desegregation plans cannot be limited to the walk-in school."[16]

Essentially, the *Green* and *Swann* decisions were aimed at reprimanding southern school officials who had evaded, at all costs, their responsibility to dismantle the dual system of separate and unequal schools. But the most significant result of this stone-walling on the part of school officials and the ensuing court decisions was that they diminished the extent to which parental choice would be factored into school desegregation remedies, particularly those in the South, for years to come. Between 1970 and 1976, hundreds of mandatory reassignment or "forced busing" plans were implemented.

School desegregation remedies in the North and West were far less extreme and often relied on voluntary, choice-oriented policies. In the North, segregated schools had not been mandated by law—at least not since the 19th century—but resulted instead from residential segregation. The distinction between southern, state-sanctioned ("de jure") segregation and northern "de facto" segregation—which came about without official state enforcement—meant that the rulings that radically altered school assignment patterns in the South in the 1970s did not affect the North.

To make matters more difficult, northern metropolitan areas were more likely than their southern counterparts to be divided into several small school districts, each serving a racially and socioeconomically homogeneous community. Countywide school districts, encompassing suburban areas and several different neighborhoods, were common in the South but rare in the North.

In 1967 the U.S. Commission on Civil Rights looked at racial segregation in public schools in 15 major northern cities and found that three-fourths of the African-American students residing in these cities attended predominantly black schools. In 9 of the 15 cities, more than half of these students attended schools that were 90 to 100 percent black.[17]

In 1973 the Supreme Court expanded its definition of de jure segregation to encompass almost any action a school board might take that resulted in racially imbalanced schools. The Court ruled in *Keyes v. School District No. 1* that, although neither the state of Colorado nor the Denver school district had mandated separate schools for white and black or Hispanic students, formal actions on the part of the school board had created and perpetuated a highly segregated system. These "formal actions" included building a new segregated school in the city's small, isolated black neighborhood. The school board had also allowed white students to transfer out of schools in integrated neighborhoods through an optional zoning program in which they could choose a predominantly white school farther from their home, thereby accelerating resegregation.[18]

Although only about 37 percent of the black students enrolled in the Denver schools were directly affected by these actions of the school board, the Court called for a districtwide remedy because "the practice of concentrating Negroes in certain schools" or building a school "with conscious knowledge that it would be a segregated school" has the reciprocal effect of keeping other nearby schools predominantly white. "In short, common sense dictates the conclusion that racially inspired school board actions have an impact beyond the particular schools that are the subjects of those actions."[19]

The *Keyes* decision helped to spell out the legal requirements for school desegregation cases involving northern and western school districts. The Court sent a strong message that a state or district could be found guilty of de jure segregation even in the absence of an official segregation policy. But the *Keyes* decision did not go so far as to rule that de facto segregation called for the same remedy as de jure segregation, despite arguments made by civil rights lawyers that all segregation, whatever its cause, was a violation of the 14th Amendment.

In a separate concurring opinion in the *Keyes* case, Justice William O. Douglas argued that the Court had not gone far enough and that the legal distinction between de facto and de jure segregation could no longer be justified:

In decreeing remedial requirements for the Charlotte/Mecklenburg school district, *Swann* dealt with a metropolitan, urbanized area in which the basic causes of segregation were generally similar to those in all sections of the country, and also largely irrelevant to the existence of historic, state-imposed segregation at the time of the *Brown* decision.[20]

He cited several ways in which states aid or abet individual choices that lead to residential segregation—e.g., "restrictive covenants" that limit certain residential areas to whites only, or government funding that encourages urban development agencies to build racial ghettos.

Ultimately, Douglas argued, it did not matter whether the state formally imposed segregation or simply sanctioned the individual decisions that led to it. But Douglas was in the minority, and the de jure/de facto distinction remained, making integration efforts in the North and West far more difficult than those in the South. Despite several well-publicized cases in northern and western cities—including Boston, Seattle, and Los Angeles—school desegregation policy never had the dramatic impact on school enrollments in these regions that it did in the South.

Between 1968 and 1980, while southern school districts were transformed from the most racially segregated to the least segregated in the country, the majority of school districts in the North did nothing to overcome segregation—at most, they instituted small, voluntary, choice-oriented transfer plans, frequently called majority-to-minority transfer plans.

While these voluntary desegregation plans were not as easily manipulated by segregationists as the southern freedom of choice plans, they placed an incredible burden on black students, who had to travel long distances, often without school-district buses, to get from all-black neighborhoods to schools in all-white ones. But, according to Rossell, significant numbers of black students—as many as 25 percent of the black students in a given district—"got on a bus at their own expense to go to a school across town."[21]

A number of these voluntary transfer plans still exist in northern districts that have never experienced court-ordered deseg-

LEVELS OF DESEGREGATION BY REGION
FOR BLACK STUDENTS, 1968–1988

	PERCENT OF BLACKS	PERCENT IN MAJORITY WHITE SCHOOLS			
	1988	1968	1972	1976	1988
SOUTH	26.3	19.1	45.1	42.9	43.5
BORDER	19.4	28.4	39.9	40.8	40.4
MIDWEST	11.0	22.7	29.7	30.5	29.9
NORTHEAST	12.4	33.2	27.5	20.1	22.7
WEST	5.8	27.8	32.6	33.2	32.9

regation. Although these plans vary considerably in the kinds of school choices they provide and the amount of integration they achieve, a few notable transfer plans have made tremendous inroads in bringing black, white, and Hispanic students together. In St. Louis, for example, the nation's largest "interdistrict" voluntary transfer plan allows African-American students who live in the city to choose predominantly white schools in one of 16 suburban school districts. Under a 1983 district court settle-

PERCENTAGE OF WHITE STUDENTS IN THE SCHOOL
OF THE AVERAGE HISPANIC STUDENT, 1970–1988,
U.S. AND REGIONS

REGION	1970	1980	1988	CHANGE
SOUTH	33.4	29.5	27.5	−5.9
BORDER	80.2	66.4	59.0	−21.2
NORTHEAST	27.5	27.0	25.7	−1.8
MIDWEST	63.6	51.9	48.7	−14.9
WEST	53.2	39.8	34.4	−18.8
U.S. TOTAL	43.8	35.5	32.0	−11.8

Tables from Gary Orfield and Franklin Monfort, *Status of School Desegregation: Next Generation.* Report to the National School Boards Association (Alexandria, Va.: National School Boards Association, 1992).

ment agreement between the St. Louis Public Schools and the suburban districts, suburban schools with enrollments that are less than 25 percent black are required to accept black transfer students. The state, which was found guilty of discrimination against African-American students, must pay for student transportation as well as a suburban school "incentive fee" equivalent to the districts' per-pupil expenditures for each transfer student. Currently 13,000 African-American students attend the suburban school of their choice through this interdistrict program.[22]

While transfer plans of this magnitude are rare, the trend in school desegregation policy in the last 15 years, even in the South and especially in urban areas, has shifted away from mandatory student reassignment plans toward voluntary transfer plans and toward another popular alternative designed to achieve desegregation: magnet schools.

MAGNET SCHOOLS

Social scientists who study school desegregation continue to disagree about the impact of mandatory student reassignment plans, or "forced busing," on white student enrollment. Some are certain that mandatory plans lead to massive white flight, particularly by high-income white families. Others point to cases of heavy white flight in urban school districts that never implemented mandatory desegregation plans, especially Chicago and Atlanta, or continued white flight from cities that abandoned mandatory busing plans, such as Los Angeles and Norfolk.

Although it's impossible to generalize about the relationship between white flight and mandatory desegregation plans because of the many variables involved, it cannot be denied that "forced busing" plans were never politically popular. Although school districts had been assigning students to public schools for decades, when they began assigning students to schools in order to achieve racial balance, the practice became far less acceptable. In fact, the indignation of many white parents whose children were reassigned to desegregated schools continues to fuel the libertarians' argument for tuition voucher plans giving parents total freedom in choosing schools, including the right to send their children to one-race schools.

By the mid-1970s, school officials faced with court orders sought new methods of bringing African-American, white, and Hispanic students together without alienating white parents by assigning their children to what were considered "inferior" minority schools. According to Gary Orfield, almost all school desegregation plans created or revised since 1980 have included some element of parental choice and educational reform, and many have relied exclusively on this strategy.[23]

The most popular method of desegregating students via parental choice is through the use of magnet schools, which provide distinct educational programs—either a curricular theme, such as math/science or performing arts, or an instructional alternative like Montessori—designed to attract students of different races or ethnic backgrounds. The idea is to create schools that offer an enhanced and engaging educational program that parents of all races prefer to their neighborhood schools.

Magnet schools became increasingly popular in the North during the early 1970s, just a few years after southern school districts were forced to abandon their "freedom of choice" plans and in the midst of the alternative education movement. In fact, the early designers of urban magnet schools were influenced by the growing popularity of alternative schools as well as by the prestige of such specialty or exam schools as Boston Latin, Bronx Science, and Chicago's Lane Tech, which were all established examples of high-quality urban public schools. Thus, in many cities the alternative schools movement coincided with the push toward voluntary school desegregation through the use of magnet schools. And while the primary goal of magnet schools was to desegregate, they offered programs that made them highly distinct from traditional neighborhood schools.

The history of judicial rulings clearly shows the double purpose served by magnet schools. In 1972, when Minneapolis was ordered to desegregate its schools, the federal district court exempted the city's four alternative schools from the desegregation order because they had already attracted an integrated student body. This was the first decision sanctioning "magnet" or specialized schools for desegregation purposes. In the *Keyes* case, in 1973, the Supreme Court confirmed the use of magnet schools as a viable part of the desegregation remedy in Denver. And again in 1975, the Court permitted the use of magnet schools for desegregation purposes in Houston.[24]

The ease with which alternative schools were incorporated into desegregation plans created what educational historian Joel Spring calls "one of those ironic twists that occur in history." According to Spring, "In the 1970s, alternative schools, which in the late 1960s had been considered part of the radical reaction to the educational establishment, became a method for avoiding forced busing for integration. The existence of alternative, or magnet, schools allowed school systems to use voluntary methods of desegregating."[25]

During the late 1970s and early 1980s, the creation of magnet schools accelerated. According to a federally funded study, by the 1981–82 school year 1,020 magnet schools had been established in 138 school districts. This survey also found that magnet schools were located almost exclusively in large urban school districts. By 1982–83 one-third of the nation's 275 largest school districts had at least one magnet school.[26]

Experts say it is difficult to give an accurate count of the total number of magnet school programs nationwide because, as with alternative schools, some programs involve an entire school while others are "schools within schools." Further complicating the problem, some school districts can't distinguish their own magnets from nonmagnets and frequently confound magnet schools with alternative schools.[27]

Studies of urban school districts conducted by Rolf K. Blank at the Council of Chief State School Officers suggest that the number of magnet schools continued to increase throughout the 1980s. Between 1983 and 1990 the average urban school district experienced a more than 50 percent increase in the number of students enrolled in magnet school programs: from about 6,000 in 1983 to 10,300 in 1989. Today virtually every urban school district offers magnet school options, and approximately 20 percent of the students who attend public high schools in large urban districts are enrolled in magnet schools. Data from 15 school districts in different regions of the country reveal that between 1983 and 1989 each district added an average of 10 magnet schools. Total magnet school enrollment now includes one-third or more of all students in Buffalo, Cincinnati, Kankakee (Illinois), St. Paul, San Diego, and Seattle.[28]

One of the most obvious reasons for the increase in the number of magnet schools is the availability of federal grant money for these programs. Beginning in 1976 with an amendment to the Emergency School Aid Act (ESAA)—a special aid program for school districts in the process of desegregating—the federal government authorized grants to support the planning and implementation of magnet schools. At that time, only 14 school districts applied for federal magnet school funding; in 1980 more than 100 applied.

In 1981 Congress passed the Education Consolidation and Improvement Act, which essentially incorporated ESAA and the magnet school amendment into a large block-grant program known as Chapter 2. According to some policy analysts, school desegregation funds suffered the worst cuts under this consolidation act, because as states gained more autonomy in how they spent federal block-grant money they channeled federal funds into other programs. Funding for magnet school programs alone dropped from $400 million in 1981 to $25 million in 1982.[29]

The Magnet School Assistance Program, passed by Congress in 1984, has increased federal funding; over the past eight years annual spending has fluctuated between $75 million and $113 million.[30] For 1992, federal funding for magnet schools was $120 million, awarded to 45 school districts.[31] About one-third of the school districts that have applied for the two-year grants under the Magnet School Assistance Program have actually received federal aid. In order to be eligible for these funds, districts must maintain close to a 50 percent white enrollment in magnet schools.[32] But this guideline can be difficult to meet, particularly in many urban school districts where white students often make up less than 20 percent of the student population. In New York's District 4, where less than 1 percent of the resident students are white, the district has recruited white students from several of the city's other 31 community school districts to qualify for federal funds.

HOW A SCHOOL BECOMES A MAGNET

The guidelines for federal magnet school funding have helped shape the design and scope of these schools of choice. Four characteristics predominate:

1. a special curricular theme or method of instruction
2. a role in desegregating students within a district
3. a choice by student and parent
4. access to students beyond a regular attendance zone.

In 1991 the U.S. Department of Education commissioned a three-year national study to count the total number of magnet schools, assess their themes, and evaluate their success in desegregating students. Until this study is complete, nationwide data on magnet school themes will remain limited. However, a 1982 Department of Education national survey of 300 magnet schools found that a full 28 percent of these schools were "fundamental" or "academics first" magnets—a theme also popular among public alternative schools at that time. The second most prevalent theme among the surveyed magnet schools was "fine arts," which included 14 percent of the schools. Tied for third were "vocational/career" magnets and the "individualized" or self-directed learning programs, at 11 percent each. The "math/science" theme ranked fourth, with 10 percent, and "multicultural/bilingual" was fifth, with 9 percent.[33]

More recent data, from surveys of individual districts, point to an increase in magnet programs focusing on math, science, and computers. In a late-1980s survey of magnet schools in 20 randomly selected districts across the country, Rossell found that these programs accounted for 11 percent of the elementary and middle schools surveyed and 19 percent of all high schools—in fact, science/aviation/engineering/computers was the most prevalent offering at the high school level.[34]

Rossell notes that although the elementary and middle school programs tend to be curriculum-oriented and high school programs vocational or career-oriented, there is some overlap. Performing arts and math/science/computer programs seem to be equally popular at all grade levels.[35]

In most large urban districts, many magnet programs are available to students. A closer look at one such district, San Diego City Schools, reveals the breadth of offerings. Currently under a court order to desegregate, San Diego operates a total of 46 magnet schools—31 at the elementary level and 15 at the secondary level. The district's 125,000 students represent a range of ethnic groups—about 35 percent white, 29 percent Hispanic, 16 percent African-American, 8 percent Filipino, 8 percent Indochinese, and 4 percent "other," including Pacific Islanders and Chinese-Americans. A total of 35,000 students—nearly a third of the entire district—are enrolled in magnet schools, which have a mandated minimum of 22 percent white enrollment.[36]

Some of San Diego's most successful magnet programs are the following:

Math/Science/Computer Magnets are the most popular, with a combined enrollment of approximately 5,250 students in three elementary and four secondary schools. One junior high school (grades 7–9) features "college status" science labs with lasers, spectrophotometers, phasecontrast/video microscopes, and a planetarium. Another secondary school (grades 7–12) offers programming courses in Logo, Basic, FORTRAN, and Pascal, as well as computer courses in desktop publishing, computer music, and digital electronics.

International Baccalaureate Magnets offer a rigorous college-preparatory curriculum based on a European educational program. Classes in the IB schools emphasize "writing across the curriculum" to hone thinking and communications skills—students complete written assignments in *all* classes, including math and science courses, where they may be asked to write a research paper on a particular scientist or mathematical theory. Most high school students enrolled in IB earn college credit from their advanced courses. Those who complete all the IB requirements receive a special "honors" high school diploma. Three elementary schools, one junior high, and one high school—with a total enrollment of 4,460—offer the IB curriculum.

Arts Magnets provide a wide range of fine and performing arts programs. Approximately 4,370 students attend three arts elementary schools—a music conservatory, a drama and dance academy, and a fine arts workshop—and one secondary school (grades 4–12) for the creative and performing arts.

Business Magnets include a "career awareness" elementary school and three high school programs that focus on business administration, industrial arts, and graphic arts. The business administration high school offers specialized courses in accounting, finance, and computer applications. These four schools serve approximately 1,720 students.

Language Magnets offer either language immersion or bilingual classrooms to 1,300 San Diego students. Three elementary school immersion magnet programs provide total language immersion —every subject taught in either Spanish or French, with a gradual transition to English in the upper grades. The bilingual programs provide instruction in Spanish and English and therefore attract both primary-Spanish and primary-English speakers.[37]

In addition to these popular offerings, San Diego has experimented with a few innovative programs in recent years, including an academy for literature and writing—where students use computers to learn to write—and a "school of the future" focusing on international business and government, with particular attention paid to Pacific Rim countries.

Magnet school offerings in San Diego and other cities point up the wide range of school choices available within the public sector and underline the importance of developing creative and imaginative programs that will enlist a broad range of parents in achieving the "common good" goal of bringing children of different races and ethnicities together.

ACCESS ISSUES—WHO ATTENDS MAGNET SCHOOLS?

Unlike the alternative public schools that were frequently founded through the grass-roots efforts of interested parents, magnet schools were generally created as a result of court-ordered desegregation plans or school board efforts to avoid desegregation suits. In most situations, a number of factors make magnet schools appear more distinguished than neighborhood schools, and keep the demand for these choice programs extremely high.

First, magnet schools are typically created within school districts already implementing some form of desegregation plan. District officials often add magnets to existing mandatory reassignment plans to provide an alternative to forced busing for white families who might otherwise flee the public schools. Magnet schools, therefore, are purposely intended to be more popular than the nonmagnet schools to which students are normally assigned in a desegregation plan, and school districts will spend an enormous amount of money promoting magnet schools and advertising their offerings.

In her recent study, Rossell found that districts prepared elaborate, detailed booklets, leaflets, and newsletters with enticing descriptions of their magnet programs: the arts magnet that "produces an extensive calendar of art events," the science magnet where "microcomputers are a part of the regular curriculum," or the Montessori magnet where "children enjoy mastery and feel a real sense of accomplishment." The regular neighborhood schools are only occasionally described in these booklets.[38] The Los Angeles Unified School District's magnet school booklet, titled *Choices*, describes the Administration of Justice and Law Magnet School as a place designed for "young men and women who wish to pursue careers in law, police science, criminology, forensics and related fields." To "enrich" the classroom experiences of students at this magnet, the booklet informs prospective applicants, the school is affiliated with the prestigious Los Angeles law firm of Baker, Hostetler, McCutchen & Black.[39]

In some cities, magnet schools are advertised regularly on television and radio in an effort to reach as many parents and students as possible. While these efforts help magnet schools attract students of different races and ethnic backgrounds, educators in nonmagnet public schools often feel that this media hype undercuts other viable programs. One teacher from a neighborhood school in St. Louis noted that, with all the promotion for the magnet schools, "people get the impression now that the neighborhood city school is the last place you want to be."[40]

The second factor favoring magnet schools is the special categorical funding they receive from state education departments and many local districts because of the political support for desegregation through choice as opposed to "forced busing." These extra state and local dollars, in addition to those flowing from the federal Magnet School Assistance Program, mean that the vast majority of magnet schools in the country enjoy certain amenities only money can buy: smaller class sizes, extra equipment for science labs and art supplies, and specialized training for teachers. Rossell's study reveals that additional instructional equipment is typically the single biggest item in a magnet school budget, but the specialized teacher training is also costly.[41]

Rolf Blank found that the average magnet school spends about $200 more per pupil each year than a regular neighborhood school. But this funding gap between magnet and nonmagnet schools varies radically by state and school district. Blank found, for instance, that magnet schools in Houston spend from $400 to $1,300 more per student than nonmagnet schools.[42]

According to a study by the Chicago Panel on Public School Policy and Finance, during the 1988–89 school year the Chicago

Public Schools spent an average of $2,304 per pupil on those schools with less than 30 percent low-income students, including most of the city's magnet schools. Meanwhile, the district spent an average of $1,995 on the neighborhood schools with between 90 and 99 percent low-income students, even though these schools were supposed to receive supplementary funds for those very students.[43]

In addition to promotional campaigns and extra resources, the third, and probably the most important, factor that makes magnet schools appear more distinguished than regular neighborhood schools is that they tend to enroll many of the most academically successful students in the district. This process of enrolling high-achieving students in magnet schools is called "creaming"—recruiting the top students for the "elite" schools, while leaving the hardest-to-educate in the neighborhood nonmagnet schools. According to the survey of magnet schools funded by the Department of Education in the early 1980s, about one-third of all magnet schools use selective criteria such as grades, tests, or auditions for admittance. The study also found that this degree of selectivity gave magnets a higher status in their communities than nonmagnet schools.[44] As one Chicago neighborhood elementary school principal put it, magnet schools "can select their staff and their children and they get extra money, so of course they look good. It would be an embarrassment if they didn't."[45]

Blank's more recent work, however, using magnet school admissions data from 15 school districts, suggests that the percentage of magnet schools using "highly" or "very" selective criteria as the basis for admission declined between 1983 and 1989. He found that in some cities, including Rochester, New York, and New York City, a growing number of secondary magnet schools are "moderately selective" and try to match magnet selection with the overall distribution of student achievement and test scores for the district.[46]

In New York City's new career magnet high schools, high test scores and grade point averages are used to select half of the student body. A lottery is used to select the other half, with one-sixth of these places set aside for students with low test scores, one-sixth for above-average students, and four-sixths for students with average scores.

A recent study of the effect of these career magnets on student performance demonstrates that students who were randomly admitted to the programs benefited greatly from the experience, especially in comparison to students of similar backgrounds who "lost the lottery" and were not offered seats in these schools. Robert L. Crain, Amy L. Heebner, and Yiu-Pong Si of Teachers College, Columbia University, found that those admitted through the lottery (1) were less likely to drop out of school at the transition point from junior to senior high school, (2) showed an improvement in reading scores, and (3) earned more credits toward graduation than their traditional public school counterparts.[47]

Despite these positive results, New York City's 133 career magnet programs represent just one tier in a hierarchy of prestigious and less-prestigious schools of choice. Seats in these career schools, for instance, are not nearly as coveted as spots in the city's highly competitive exam schools.

Furthermore, a two-year study by Donald Moore and Suzanne Davenport of the Chicago educational research center Designs for Change examined magnet high schools in Boston, Chicago, New York, and Philadelphia.[48] They found that even when magnet schools did not use selection criteria, they tended to enroll a self-selected group of higher-achieving students. This meant that the students most at risk of failure were left in highly segregated neighborhood or zoned high schools that often had to make do without the extra resources given to magnet schools, and without the best teachers and the most motivated students. Moore and Davenport cited several reasons for this self-selection process. First, a limited supply of seats in the magnet schools fosters competition among families. Second, the success of the magnet schools creates a commonly held perception that the schools are designed for high-achieving students only and this discourages lower-achieving students from applying.

Making matters worse, the researchers found, many families do not understand the magnet school application process:

> The majority of students either did not apply or filled out an admissions form with little understanding of the complexities that would determine their chances of success. Those who did not apply were often unaware of the brief periods during which applications were accepted, which in some instances amounted to a single week or day. Many who did apply did not know much about (Liberman) the nature and quality of the specific options available, about the previous coursework they should have taken to qualify themselves for a particular option, about the odds of admission to particular programs, or about the strategies that brought success in the admissions process.[49]

Families with time and personal connections are therefore in a better position to master the written and unwritten rules of the application process and to secure their children's admission to a desired school. Parents who are poor, move frequently, or do not speak English are less likely to help their children negotiate the magnet school choice and admissions process.[50]

Furthermore, the school districts' "informal counseling" serves to channel the high-achieving, middle-income students into the higher-status magnet schools. Moore and Davenport found, for instance, that certain junior high counselors establish ties with particular magnet high schools and attempt to build a reputation for their schools through their success in placing students in prestigious magnet high schools. Thus, it is in the interest of these junior high counselors to recommend only those students they are certain will succeed. And magnet high schools often selectively recruit students from particular junior highs—public schools in moderate-income neighborhoods or private schools. "These practices, often based on a network of established relationships between junior high counselors and high school recruiters, [work] to the disadvantage of schools serving many students at risk."[51]

The resulting tendency of magnet schools to exclude all but the highest-achieving students or those with the most involved parents raises important issues of access and equity, and calls into question all efforts to compare the "quality" of magnet schools to that of nonmagnets. Despite Blank and Douglas A. Archbald's finding that an increasing number of magnet schools are trying to attract students based on interest, not ability level, it appears that there may be a correlation between the two.[52] Virtually all of the research comparing academic achievement in magnet and regular schools shows that students in magnet schools have higher test scores. Many of these studies, however, fail to consider the students' backgrounds and prior school achievement.[53] The small body of research that tracks individual achievement over time and controls for background and prior performance shows a small independent positive effect on test scores of magnet students.[54]

Magnet schools' success as desegregation tools is also questionable. Magnet schools in urban districts, many of which are 75 percent or more nonwhite, tend to enroll a disproportionate number of white students in order to maintain a desired racial balance, often close to 50 percent white. This also means that nonmagnet urban schools become increasingly segregated.

There is also some evidence that the high status of certain magnet schools—reputations born of perceived selectivity and high-achieving students—is more "magnetic" to prospective students and their parents than any specific theme or curricular offering. For instance, surveys have found that as many as 87 percent of parents with children enrolled in magnet schools did not know the theme of their child's school. The parents' attraction to the magnet schools was based on a general perception of magnets as "good schools."[55] And what parents perceive to be "good" schools is often the product of racial attitudes that lead them to assume schools with a higher percentage of white students are "better," as are schools located in a "good"—e.g., white and affluent—neighborhood. Researchers have found, for instance, that magnet schools located in inner-city, predominantly African-American or Latino neighborhoods are often perceived to be of a lower quality than those with identical programs located in white, middle-class neighborhoods. In 1989, seats for white students went unfilled at Los Angeles's inner-city magnet schools while similar magnet programs in the city's predominantly white neighborhoods had long waiting lists.[56] In fact, many so-called magnet schools in South-Central and East Los Angeles have no white students at all.

Gary Orfield notes in *Must We Bus?* that even "expensive 'magnet schools' located in the ghetto whose education programs are far superior to those offered in all-white schools have found it difficult to attract volunteer transfer students."[57] In a recent study of student choice patterns among magnet elementary schools in Montgomery County, Maryland, Jeffrey Henig found that "in spite of officials' intent to structure incentives to promote integration, white families tended to prefer schools with a lower proportion of minorities and minority families tended to opt for schools in lower-income, high-minority neighborhoods."[58]

These issues raise important questions about whether or not even the "best" schools of choice offer equitable and workable solutions to the persistent problem of racial isolation in American education, particularly in the urban centers. What follows is an example of how equitable desegregation plans can be implemented in a way that incorporates parental choice.

THE POTENTIAL OF MAGNET SCHOOLS

There are several parallels to be drawn between effective alternative public school programs, such as New York City's District 4, and effective school desegregation plans that include magnet schools and parental choice. These parallels are best illustrated by a description of what is known as a "controlled choice" desegregation plan.

In Cambridge, Massachusetts, site of the nation's oldest and most famous controlled choice plan, each of the city's 14 elementary schools houses two to four alternative or magnet "schools within schools." As with junior high students in New York's District 4, every elementary school student in Cambridge is guaranteed a place in a school of choice because there are no "neighborhood" or "zoned" schools. As in District 4, all parents and students must go through the choice process, guided by school district personnel who meet with families to discuss the various schools and programs.

But the important distinction between Cambridge and District 4 is that the controlled choice plan in Cambridge is, first and foremost, a school desegregation plan. In the 1970s, Cambridge school board members looked across the Charles River to Boston and saw the violence and hatred generated by mandatory desegregation. Determined to avoid a similar court order, the Cambridge board, along with teachers, parents, and community members, designed an innovative parental choice plan that would guarantee all students in the racially diverse district a seat in an integrated magnet school of their choice. What started as a loosely structured open enrollment plan designed to fend off a mandatory busing order soon became much more than a "desegregation plan." By 1981 the current controlled choice plan had been enacted, and it proved to be an effective mechanism for school reform, popular with parents, students, and teachers.[59]

The Cambridge elementary schools include grades kindergarten through eight, and one high school serves the entire district. When it is time for parents to enroll their children for kindergarten, they meet with a counselor at the district's Parent Information Center. If a parent cannot get to the Parent Information Center, a center representative will go to them. Multilingual counselors go to housing projects and hospitals; they comb local Head Start programs in search of the parents of incoming kindergartners.

After parents are informed of the different magnet school programs available in the district—programs ranging from creative writing to fundamental or "basic skills," to open, unstructured classrooms, to multicultural arts, computer-oriented curriculum, and bilingual Spanish immersion—and have visited schools, they list their top three school choices. Then the district's student-assignment officer and parent counselors go to work to ensure that each school ends up with a student body that loosely reflects the city's racial makeup: 50 percent white, 30 percent African-American, 13 percent Hispanic, and 7 percent Asian.

Although the schools' curricula and instructional methods vary, popular magnet programs are replicated in more than one school so that no one school has a monopoly on a well-liked theme. This duplication of popular programs means that the district is better able to assure racial balance in all schools, and parents are more likely to get the magnet school of their choice.

Like District 4's choice plan, Cambridge's controlled choice program operates in a single public school district that has an obligation to serve all the children who live within its boundaries. Therefore, when one of the district's magnet schools fails to attract enough students, district officials work with the teachers to improve the school instead of leaving it to slowly "go out of business"—as unpopular schools in a deregulated, free-market model of educational choice would do. The district superintendent and board of education are responsible for assuring that a minimum level of educational quality is maintained in *all* schools at *all* times. In addition, because the students stay within the district, they are all provided free, public transportation to their school of choice.

Cambridge, like District 4, allows teachers, program directors, and building principals relative autonomy to run their programs as they see fit. Because each of the magnet schools-within-a-school must attract a new racially diverse kindergarten class each year and try to retain these same students through the eighth grade, the educators at the school are by necessity very responsive to parents. Such school-site autonomy—along with principal leadership and coherence between the magnet theme and the curriculum and staffing—was cited as a critical characteristic of successful magnet schools in the nationwide study of magnet schools in the early 1980s.[60]

The fact that the Cambridge plan allows for all of the benefits of magnet school education without any of the obvious drawbacks could explain why test scores there have continued to rise steadily since controlled choice was introduced 13 years ago. In 1991, 76 percent of Cambridge's third-, sixth-, and ninth-graders passed the reading, math, and writing sections of the Massachusetts Basic Skills Test. In 1987 only 62 percent had passed these exams. Also, between 1981 and 1988, Scholastic Aptitude Test score averages in the district rose by 89 points to a combined 859, but fell back to 805 by 1991.[61] Still another sign of success is the 10 percent increase in the proportion of school-age children in Cambridge attending public schools since the program began.[62]

Controlled choice programs now exist in at least 20 school districts, including Montclair, New Jersey; Richmond, California; and 16 of Massachusetts's 436 school districts. In Boston, the largest district to attempt controlled choice as an alternative to mandatory student reassignment, the district has been divided into three "zones." Each zone is operated like a mini school district, with families choosing among the schools in their zones. In March 1992 the board of the Indianapolis Public Schools voted to transform the district's current desegregation plan into a controlled choice program within the next few years.[63] Still, the Cambridge model of controlled choice is not without its shortcomings. For instance, the 1992 Carnegie Foundation report on school choice points out that despite extra funding and efforts, and despite the fact that the 14 elementary schools are racially balanced, "poor, immigrant, non-English speakers remain relatively isolated in one or two schools, and minority students are generally overrepresented in special education and underrepresented in honors programs."[64] This suggests that while controlled choice plans may have succeeded in minimizing inequality inherent in choice plans with choosers and nonchoosers, more attention needs to be paid to tracking issues and to the integration of language-minority students.

Furthermore, controlled choice is not cheap. The Massachusetts State Department of Education has spent millions of extra desegregation dollars to pay for parent information centers and extra transportation costs. In Cambridge alone, the annual extra cost of the parent information center and staff development to revitalize unpopular schools of choice exceeds $500,000 a year. Transportation costs for the 1991–92 school year were $407,378. Even before these costs are added in, Cambridge ranks near the top in the state in per-pupil expenditures—more than $9,000 for the 1992–93 school year.[65] The Richmond Unified School District went bankrupt in 1991 and had to be taken over by the California State Department of Instruction, in part because of the high cost of the district's magnet programs.

But what makes controlled choice plans worth the extra cost is their potentially beneficial effects on school districts: They may well enhance the common good and the quality of education provided, and contribute to individual student growth and fulfillment. Charles V. Willie, a Harvard University expert on school desegregation and controlled choice and a special adviser to the Boston Public Schools, believes that an education plan that is "fair and just requires student body diversity, controlled choice, and school improvement strategies, not one or the other but all three."[66] He lauds controlled choice for the balance of freedom and control it allows communities in addressing critical issues of equity and school improvement.

Hence, controlled choice plans strike a delicate balance between parents' rights to choose appropriate educational settings for their children and society's obligation to distribute educational opportunities more equally.

SCHOOL CHOICE AND THE COMMON GOOD

This chapter has focused on how the effort to provide families with greater choice in education can dovetail with the legal and moral obligation to desegregate the public schools. Experience has shown that limited, unstructured school choice—e.g., freedom-of-choice plans or a handful of selective magnet schools—does not necessarily lead to overall integration, nor does it serve those students in greatest need. Such programs fail not only to meet the broader social goals of our society, but also to improve overall educational quality and the individual experiences of students.

This does not mean that effective school desegregation plans and worthwhile parental choice plans need be mutually exclusive. On the contrary, controlled choice programs provide evidence that school choice can be structured in a way to assure that all families have viable choices and all schools are racially balanced. The similarities between the successful choice program in New York's District 4 and Cambridge's controlled choice plan underscore many of the required ingredients for successful public-school choice programs, especially those designed to bring students of different races and cultures together:

First, all students must be guaranteed a school choice. Because these successful plans do away with "zoned" or neighborhood schools, all students are "forced" to choose a magnet or alternative program in order to enroll in an elementary school (in Cambridge) or a junior high (in District 4). Thus, successful and equitable school choice plans do not foster a system of "choosers and nonchoosers" in which a lucky minority are admitted to the popular and prestigious schools of choice while the rest are left behind in low-status neighborhood schools.

Second, a school choice plan must operate within one public school district or a union of two or more districts. This prevents public education dollars from being siphoned off to support private and religious schools or wealthy suburban districts. It also means that *all* students living within a district—or a group of unified districts—will be guaranteed a free public education. Parents need not pay an additional tuition fee for schools of choice, and precious resources do not follow high-achieving, highly motivated students to the most prestigious schools, leaving lower-achieving students behind in schools with dwindling resources. Keeping choice within the public schools and within a unified district boundary assures that each district will be forced to provide all "customers" with a school program that they like, while also helping to assure that the district has the money to do so. Also, keeping choice within the public sector assures that some measure of racial balance can be achieved within each school. Choice plans that include private schools, on the other hand, could not guarantee any racial or ethnic desegregation. In fact, most research suggests such plans would lead to greater racial isolation within the educational system.

Third, a school district's parent information center must be staffed with enough parent counselors or teachers to provide every family in the district the time and personal attention to talk about the variety of school choices, their child's particular needs, and their school preferences. Every family must gain access to schools of choice through such a center. These centers also serve another purpose. They help parents become more involved in decision making about their own children's education and provide a forum in which parents may express opinions about the district's programs. In this regard, parents in controlled choice districts engage in what Dewey called the "dialogical" process of collective problem solving and become actively involved in determining the common good.

Fourth, free and reliable public transportation must be available to every child if meaningful school choice is to occur. In some urban areas, this may be as simple as paying for older students' subway or bus tokens. For younger students in these areas, and for students in cities, suburbs, and rural communities without public transportation, school districts must provide buses to transport all children from their homes to their schools of choice. If districts fail to provide free transportation, many students—particularly those from low-income families—will be forced to attend the school nearest their home, whether or not it is their school of choice.

Fifth, districts with equitable choice plans must replicate the most popular programs in various schools-within-schools so that no one school has a monopoly on a successful theme. This helps guarantee that all students have access to the program they desire. In a school choice program motivated by concern for equity and the common good, educators do not view themselves as competing with one another to be the "best" school with the "smartest" students, but rather they understand the importance of working collaboratively, sharing information and materials, and encouraging "good" schools to multiply.

Sixth, policymakers at the federal, state, and local levels must allow teachers and principals the flexibility and autonomy required to shape their schools and programs to meet the individual needs of the students they serve. When educators are free to provide the services tailored to the learning needs of their students, the concept of "school choice" gains real meaning. Only when educators are treated as professionals and allowed to try different and innovative pedagogical approaches will parents and students be fairly served.

Controlled choice plans that include all of these characteristics are easiest to implement in small-to-medium-size school districts. It would, no doubt, be incredibly difficult to institute a program of controlled choice in a huge urban school system, where demographics, geography, and lack of funding make the requisite innovations nearly impossible. But Boston's efforts to break the district into zones—similar in many respects to the community school districts within the larger New York City system—may show the way to providing every urban student with a viable school choice. District 4's success in working independently of the rest of the New York City public schools is encouraging.

Cambridge's plan proves that fair and equitable racial desegregation plans can also provide meaningful parental choice. Such plans ease the long-felt tension created by white resistance to "forced busing." These programs also involve parents and students from "all walks of life" in decision making and problem solving as the district creates and discontinues various alternatives.

Public-school choice programs that succeed in all of the aforementioned areas will no doubt advance the goal of education for the common good. Such plans fulfill Dewey's expectations for education to help society "overcome the divisions between families and schools, nature and daily life, and most important, between different classes of people. . . ."[67] And they do so without sacrificing the goal of education for individual fulfillment.

I would argue, therefore, that a school choice plan that serves the common good and the needs of individual students cannot help but achieve the third educational objective—a better-educated work force. Yet, as the following chapters demonstrate, choice plans driven mainly by work-force needs all too often fail to consider the common good.

J ust as alternative education emerged in the 1970s as the popular way of providing families with school choice, and in the 1980s the creation of magnet schools became the primary method of offering school choice, in the 1990s new statewide choice programs—including "open enrollment," "postsecondary options," and "charter schools"—will no doubt predominate.

Conceived in the politically conservative late 1980s, these statewide plans reflect a different educational philosophy from those articulated in the alternative schools movement or the efforts to create choice-oriented desegregation. Instead of focusing exclusively on how schools can better meet the individual needs of students or help achieve a broad social goal such as racial integration, statewide choice plans are designed to infuse the free-market principle of competitiveness into public education. Driven primarily by the economic-competitive goal of education, these statewide programs more closely resemble tuition voucher plans because they tie state education money to individual student choices and thereby threaten public schools with loss of resources or extinction if they fail to attract enough students. Furthermore, some of these programs include private schools at the postsecondary level.

Two of the statewide programs described here—open enrollment and postsecondary options—were specifically designed to make school officials aware that students living within their districts were not guaranteed "customers," and that "better" schools or educational institutions could easily lure students and state educational dollars away. This intimidation was intended to make schools more responsive to the demands of their students and encourage educational excellence.

The central question, however, is whether or not all schools are able—in terms of resources, size, location, current student population, etc.—to compete in the educational marketplace. And, if not, what happens to students who cannot, for whatever geographic, economic, or personal reasons, transfer out of the least competitive districts?

Because these various statewide choice programs are relatively new, only limited data exist on whom they are serving and their effects on students or schools. Preliminary findings suggest that the mobility they afford some students may come at the expense of programs serving others. In fact, all of the five statewide programs discussed here except one—the one least driven by competitive principles—have the potential to lead to far greater inequality within the educational system.

Minnesota became the first state to implement statewide choice plans in the mid-1980s, shortly after Democratic governor Rudy Perpich unveiled his "Access to Excellence" plan for educational reform. The plan stressed improved student performance and statewide testing, increases in state aid from 65 percent of average per-pupil cost to 85 percent, and options that allowed parents and students to choose among public schools outside of their local school district and take their state per-pupil funding with them. This later came to be known as an "open enrollment" plan. The governor—sometimes referred to as the Pied Piper of school choice—also called for several programs that would allow high school students to enroll in classes outside of their assigned secondary school—in colleges, universities, job training centers, or alternative schools.[1]

As a result of this program and the passage of several other significant pieces of education legislation since 1985, Minnesota has become the national leader in statewide choice plans. What follows is a detailed description of each of Minnesota's choice programs, reviews of research findings on the impact of these statewide programs, and an overview of other states that have enacted similar legislation.

POSTSECONDARY OPTIONS

The first statewide choice legislation to pass in Minnesota, the Postsecondary Enrollment Options Act of 1985, made it possible for juniors and seniors in public high schools to attend postsecondary institutions, including public universities, community colleges, vocational-technical institutes, or two- and four-year private colleges. Provisions allow students to take nonsectarian courses on a full- or part-time basis at these institutions and receive either high school or college credit. Individual high schools can also elect to offer "college in the schools" classes, which are taught by high school teachers under the direction of a university or college professor and can be counted as a postsecondary education class. The cost of tuition, fees, and textbooks for these classes is paid by the students' school district, using the state education aid that would have been spent on the students in their regular high school. The districts pay for this out of their per-pupil state "foundation aid," which averages about $4,000 per student at the secondary level. The exact amount spent per pupil varies based on the number of classes a student takes. Thus, when students from a given district choose to attend postsecondary institutions, the district has less state education money to spend on K-12 education. After a 1991 reauthorization of the legislation, beginning in the 1993–94 school year, school districts will receive even less general education revenue for students participating in the Postsecondary Enrollment Options program.[2]

According to the Minnesota Department of Education, $5.174 million in state aid was paid by school districts to postsecondary institutions during the 1990–91 school year, with 6,675 students participating. During the 1991–92 school year, student enrollment in the program increased to 7,534, which cost high schools throughout the state close to $10 million. Interestingly enough, because the postsecondary institutions generally charge less in tuition than the state foundation aid the districts must pay back when their students participate, the program cost the state $31.42 million, only $2.2 million beyond the $29.22 million that would have been earmarked for those students through their high schools anyway.[3]

The stated purpose of the Postsecondary Enrollment Options (PSEO) plan is to encourage students to pursue a more rigorous program of study than they would normally in their local high school. Supporters argue that competition from the postsecondary institutions will encourage school districts to offer more advanced-placement and other rigorous academic courses to entice students to remain in high school. In this way, the program reflects the national "excellence" movement of the 1980s. According to Joe Nathan and Wayne Jennings, in a report on the impact of four statewide choice programs, the number of advanced-placement courses offered in the state's high schools has increased four times since 1985, at least partly as a result of the Postsecondary Enrollment Options program.[4] But the Carnegie Foundation report on school choice states that, among 497 high schools surveyed, the number of schools offering advanced placement has risen only slightly in recent years—from 125 in 1989 to 147 in 1992.[5] And Judith Pearson, in her book on choice plans in Minnesota, *The Myths of Educational Choice*, tells of one small high school where advanced courses, including physics and calculus, were cut after several students began taking classes at the nearby community college through the Postsecondary Enrollment Options plan. This meant that the students left behind in the high school, for whatever reason, were actually denied rigorous courses as a result of this plan.[6]

The program was also intended to give juniors and seniors a much wider variety of choices for course work. And it does, no doubt, for students who have access to postsecondary institutions. But in a primarily rural state like Minnesota, families that live in the more remote areas will have fewer choices than their counterparts in urban areas such as Minneapolis and St. Paul. The state offers students from families with incomes below the federal poverty line a transportation stipend of 15 cents per mile to cover the cost of commuting to a postsecondary institution. But this is far from adequate in many cases. "[The stipend] does not buy you a car that will run in the dead of a Minnesota winter," said author Judith Pearson, who is also a teacher in a northern Minnesota high school.[7] In *The Myths of Educational Choice* Pearson provides several examples of high school students who are not able to participate in the Postsecondary Options program (as this plan is generally called) or any of Minnesota's other choice plans, because they don't have transportation to their school or program of choice.

Several public school administrators and teachers, as well as the state teachers' union, objected to the initial legislation over these issues of access and equity. According to Jessie Montano of the Minnesota Department of Education, educators leveled other charges once the legislation took effect. They argued that school districts would lose crucial funds to postsecondary institutions, that high schools would lose their student leaders to postsecondary institutions, that students would choose the postsecondary institutions for courses (e.g., foreign languages) already available in the high schools, and that parents would favor the program primarily because it saved them money on college tuition and not because the high schools lacked rigorous course offerings.[8]

In response to these concerns—and to complaints from parents that high schools were not providing sufficient information about the program—legislators added several amendments to the original act. High schools are now required to provide information and counseling to students and parents interested in postsecondary options, to establish time lines within which students must notify their high schools of their intent to participate in the program, to limit student involvement in the program to no more than two years, to prohibit participating students from applying for state financial aid in addition to their Postsecondary Options stipend from their district, and to require the signature of parents for participating students under age 18.[9]

Although these amendments add more structure to the program, they fail to address many of the key equity issues, including who has access and who doesn't and what happens to students who choose not to participate. In a 1987 review of the Postsecondary Options program, Montano concluded that many of the preliminary concerns of high school educators were not substantiated. For instance, she stated that the program did not cream off the high schools' "best" students or their student leaders. In fact, she found that more than 60 percent of the participants reported their high school grade point average was either B, C, or D—though she did not mention whether the other 40 percent were A students. But Montano noted that students who were attracted to the program tended to be those who had exhausted their high school curriculum, those with high test scores but low grades, and those who wanted the experience of taking a college course.[10] Of course, one might suppose that students in the first or third category tend to be high achievers.

Montano also stated that the Postsecondary Options program was not biased against rural students who lived many miles from four-year universities. Her data from these early years of the program demonstrate that the highest participation rate was among students in high schools outside metropolitan areas and that 49 percent of the participants were enrolling in one of the state's 18 community colleges.[11]

Furthermore, she found that 90 percent of the students claimed they were learning more by taking both high school and postsecondary classes, and 87 percent of their parents said the children were studying harder for the postsecondary courses than they did for their high school classes. The problem most frequently cited by program participants was that of coordinating class schedules between the secondary and postsecondary schools. Transportation was not considered a major problem for most participating students, but there were no data concerning whether or not lack of transportation limited access for nonparticipants.[12]

Finally, Montano argued that the Postsecondary Options program did not drain high schools of needed state resources. In the first year of the program, with about 3,600 students participating, the cost for the average school district was less than 1 percent of the entire 11th- and 12th-grade foundation aid revenue from the state.[13] Although the number of program participants more than doubled in the first five years, the 11th- and 12th-grade foundation aid flowing to postsecondary institutions remained at less than 1 percent for the 1991–92 school year, according to Minnesota Department of Education estimates.[14] Still, the new funding formula for 1993 promises to make the program more expensive for high schools. According to a report by the Minnesota House of Representatives on the Postsecondary Options program, "The costs are of particular concern to districts since they are significantly higher than the costs they faced in FY 1991 for essentially the same program. . . . If PSEO participation becomes the cause of a significant loss in district revenue, districts may be in the unenviable position of balancing the needs of the district against benefits for some of its students."[15]

In a 1990 report on the Postsecondary Options program, Joe Nathan and Wayne Jennings found that the "vast majority" of the 5,500 high school students who took part in the program during the 1989–90 school year enrolled in challenging academic courses; and at many colleges, including the University of Minnesota, these students earned slightly higher grades than members of the freshman class.[16]

But the authors also observed that students from low-income families were vastly underrepresented. For instance, while 21 percent of the K-12 student population in the state is eligible for free or reduced-price lunches, only 11 percent of the students participating in the Postsecondary Options program said that their families had received some sort of public assistance in the last five years. According to the Minnesota Department of Education official in charge of transportation reimbursements for the choice programs, the state has had very few requests from low-income families for stipends to cover the cost of driving to a postsecondary institution. Although the state legislature initially appropriated $50,000 annually for transportation stipends for both the Postsecondary Options program and the Open Enrollment plan, the amount of state money requested by low-income families for the 1990–91 school year was only $11,600.

Also telling is the finding by Nathan and Jennings that more than half of the Postsecondary Options students had parents with at least some college education, and 43 percent of their fathers and 33 percent of their mothers hold the minimum of a college degree. This is much higher than the Minnesota adult population as a whole, in which only 17 percent are college graduates.[17] Because income and years of education are strongly correlated, these findings suggest students from higher-income families are participating at a greater rate.

In terms of access and participation by racial group, Nathan and Jennings reported that the percentage of nonwhite participants was 6.2 percent, lower than the state average of 9.24 percent minority students.[18]

The Nathan and Jennings survey, which had only a 67 percent response rate, did show that participating students came from the three types of residential areas in roughly equal numbers— 32 percent from urban areas, 35 percent from suburban areas, and 32 percent from rural areas.[19] These findings, though, do not take into account the total numbers of Minnesota students who dwell in each of these types of residential areas, or differences in the types of postsecondary institutions that participating students from these different areas attend. The 1993 Minnesota House of Representatives report states that school districts with no student participation tend to be those located a great distance from a postsecondary institution and are usually the smallest school districts, with average enrollments of 259. The report also found, interestingly enough, that districts with modest rates of participation (5 to 15 percent) tend to be those in close proximity to a postsecondary institution, and that districts with the highest level of participation (40 percent of their 11th- and 12th-graders) were somewhere in between.[20] Still, the report showed that not all students had access to the same postsecondary experiences. For instance, in districts with the highest participation rates, large numbers of students were enrolled in "college in the schools" classes, while in the larger districts with moderate participation rates, students were more likely to be attending universities and colleges.[21]

Furthermore, a comparison of Minneapolis–St. Paul metropolitan-area residents to non-metro-area residents demonstrates huge discrepancies in the quality of the institutions students attend, with almost ten times the number of metro students attending the University of Minnesota and two times the number of non-metro students attending technical colleges.[22]

In terms of the effects of the program on student learning, only 32 percent of the Postsecondary Options students said they were more successful in school after participating in the program. Nearly 60 percent said their school success level had remained unchanged, and 7 percent said they were less successful than before they entered the program.[23] Pearson, citing a report by the Minnesota Community College System, states that in 1989–90 half of the Postsecondary Options students who enrolled in two courses at a community college did not complete one or both courses.[24] Also, participation did not affect student expectations about future educational attainment. For instance, before entering the program, 73.3 percent of the responding participants stated that they planned to attend college or receive vocational training after high school. After participation in the program, 72.3 percent said that they planned to continue their education after high school.[25]

Obviously, more questions need to be answered before any conclusions can be drawn about the impact of the Postsecondary Options plan on the students who participate or, perhaps more important, the students who do not. It appears that students who enroll in a postsecondary institution may benefit to some small degree, but what is not clear is whether the majority of students who remain in their high schools are jeopardized by the plan. What about the students who have been tracked into "low-ability" or basic classes? Do they benefit when their high school begins offering more advanced-placement courses in an effort to retain students who would leave to enroll in postsecondary institutions? And more important, what are the obstacles that prevent larger numbers of students, particularly low-income students, from participating—geography, lack of transportation and/or information, fear of failure?

Furthermore, all postsecondary options are not equal. For rural students who have access only to technical and community colleges, the quality of their postsecondary experience, and the value of the course credits they receive, may be significantly lower than that of students with access to four-year institutions. According to Pearson, students reported that some of the courses at the community colleges were easier than those at their high schools, and they participated in the program in order to get higher grades for less work. She also notes that students have figured out that if they earn their credits through postsecondary institutions they are required to spend less time in class. "[Y]ou have to be really stupid not to figure it out. You have to spend 170 class periods at high school to get a credit and you can get the same credit at college for only 120 class periods," Pearson quotes one student as saying.[26] Meanwhile, some of the state's most selective private colleges have refused to participate in the program on the grounds that high school students are not academically or socially prepared for college work.[27]

One concern that researchers have not investigated thus far is the issue of status: high school students might participate in the program because taking a college-level class is considered more prestigious, or simply because it is deemed a novel opportunity. This would of course make it more difficult for high schools to "compete" with colleges and universities for students. If students who participate in the Postsecondary Options plan are motivated by such concerns, this form of school choice will serve these individual students well. It will not, however, serve the students who remain behind in high school courses, which will by definition have lower status and prestige.

Despite such nettlesome questions, eight other states have passed similar legislation. Arizona allows 11th- and 12th-graders to take courses for high school credit at community colleges or vocational/technical centers. Florida allows high school students to enroll in community colleges only, and Colorado permits juniors and seniors in high school to take college courses at both two- and four-year institutions, with state dollars following the students. Maine allows school districts to retain the right to decide whether or not state dollars will follow students. Both Oregon and Utah operate modified postsecondary programs, which enable a limited number of students to attend community colleges.[28] Wisconsin and New Mexico became the most recent states to enact Postsecondary Options plans, and the Mississippi legislature is currently considering such a bill.[29]

HIGH SCHOOL GRADUATION INCENTIVES AND AREA LEARNING CENTERS

In 1987 the Minnesota legislature passed measures creating two additional choice-oriented programs: High School Graduation Incentives and the Area Learning Centers. The Graduation Incentives program allows high school dropouts and other "at-risk" students between the ages of 12 and 21 to enroll in either a public high school outside their school district or an alternative educational program—public or private nonsectarian. The Area Learning Centers serve students age 16 to 21 and adults who elect to finish high school in an alternative setting. This program, like Graduation Incentives, is designed for at-risk students and high school dropouts. Students who do not live in school districts with learning centers may attend one in another district without obtaining permission from the local school board.

As with the Postsecondary Options program, state aid follows the students from the school district in which they live to their schools of choice. Students, though, must provide their own transportation.

The main purpose of these two school choice programs is to offer students who are not thriving in their assigned residential school a second chance at educational success. These programs, more than any of the other statewide school choice plans that have been enacted in the last five years, are guided by the philosophy of the alternative schools movement and the goal of education for the sake of individual growth and fulfillment. In other words, they support the view that all children can learn, but that traditional schools do not always offer the best learning environment for every student. To achieve their goals, these programs draw on Minnesota's already extensive assortment of alternative educational programs and also encourage educators to develop new alternative schools geared toward students who have not been well served in traditional schools.

A free-market philosophy that asks schools and school districts to compete for clients is not really compatible with programs such as these. School districts do not typically "compete" for the least successful students, even when these students bring state education dollars with them. In fact, at a time when below-average test scores and dropout rates get intense scrutiny in the media, it is not in a school board's best interest to hold on to students who are at risk for failure. These less successful students also tend to cost more to educate, as they often require specialized programs and a high degree of individual attention. In other words, districts may find it fiscally advantageous to let such students opt for other districts or privately run programs rather than compete for them. In addition, the Learning Center legislation's stipulation that students can transfer into a center in another school district "without permission from the school board" suggests that Minnesota's legislators realized at the outset that students assisted by this act are not generally the most sought-after.

Indeed, the limited amount of research on Graduation Incentives and Learning Centers indicates that these programs serve a different clientele from that of Postsecondary Options and that their impact on participating students appears to be quite positive. For instance, Nathan and Jennings in their 1990 survey found that, unlike the Postsecondary Options program, whose enrollment had a smaller percentage of low-income students than the state's average for students, Graduation Incentives and the Learning Centers served a significantly larger number of students from low-income families. In fact, 38 percent of the students enrolled in private nonsectarian alternative schools through the Graduation Incentives program were from low-income families, as were 30 percent of the students enrolled in public schools through the program. Similarly, 37 percent of the students who opted for the Learning Centers were from low-income homes.[30]

According to a recent report by Policy Studies Associates in Washington, D.C., these two programs also serve a more racially diverse group of students: 57 percent of the students opting for the private alternative programs under Graduation Incentives are racial or ethnic minorities.[31] This data coincides with Nathan and Jennings's finding that nearly 88 percent of the participants in the private alternative programs reside in urban areas, where the highest concentration of African-American, Hispanic, Laotian, Hmong, and Vietnamese students are found.[32]

Students of color represent only about 9 percent of those opting to attend a different public school through Graduation Incentives and only 8 percent of those participating in the Learning Centers program.[33] These statistics reflect the fact that most of the Area Learning Centers are located in suburban or rural neighborhoods. Information concerning the differences between the public and private, urban and suburban alternative programs is not offered in this report, and no such evaluation of the quality of any of these programs has yet been made.

Students participating in the Graduation Incentives and the Learning Centers tend to come from families in which parents have fewer years of education than those in the postsecondary plan. While 50 percent of the Postsecondary Options students in the 1990 report came from families with one parent who had some college experience, less than 25 percent of the Graduation Incentives students and the Learning Center students had even one parent with college experience.[34] According to the 1992 Policy Studies Associates report, 26 percent of Learning Center students, as opposed to 19 percent in private alternative schools through Graduation Incentives, reported that their mothers had attended college.[35]

Students in the Graduation Incentives program were also more likely than other students in either the Learning Centers or the Postsecondary Options program to state that finding transportation to and from their schools of choice presented a major or minor problem.

The Policy Studies Associates report offers insight into some of the reasons why the students participating in these two programs did not succeed in their previous schools. Only 28 percent of the students attending private alternatives through Graduation Incentives said that the classes in their former school had been interesting or challenging. Similarly, 27 percent said that their teachers at their previous schools were interested in them, and only 31 percent reported getting praise from their teachers after working hard on an assignment. Responses from students attending Area Learning Centers indicated slightly better experiences, with 36 percent reporting that their former school had been interesting, 37 percent stating that their teachers had been interested in them, and 44 percent indicating that when they worked hard on an assignment their teachers had praised them.[36]

These data make it clear that the Graduation Incentives and Learning Centers programs serve a lower-income and more racially diverse population of students who were more dissatisfied with their previous schools than those participating in the Postsecondary Options plan. And in terms of the effectiveness of these programs, participants were much more likely than their Postsecondary Options counterparts to say that the program had a positive effect on their performance. While only 32 percent of the Postsecondary Options students said they were more successful after participation, 73 percent of the Graduation Incentive students and about 85 percent of the Learning Center students saw real results.

Similarly, while the Postsecondary Options students stated that the program had not affected their expectations about college and career training, the Graduation Incentives and the Learning Centers programs appear to have had a major impact on student college aspirations: The number who said they planned to pursue higher education climbed, for example, from 6 percent to 41 percent among students enrolled for one or two years in a private alternative school under the Learning Centers program alone. Furthermore, the percentage of students in the public alternative schools as well as those participating in the Graduation Incentives program who said they planned to go to college after high school doubled.[37] The Policy Studies Associates report also found that the percentage of students attending a private alternative school through the Graduation Incentives program who said they expected to graduate from high school soared from 22 percent before participation in the program to 64 percent after enrollment. For students in the Area Learning Centers, the number of students who thought they would graduate from high school went from 26 percent before enrollment in the centers to 49 percent after enrollment.

Once again, more data are needed concerning who these participants are, why they did not succeed in a traditional high school, and why the Graduation Incentives and Learning Centers programs seem to work. Nathan and Jennings do provide a short profile of one student who entered a Learning Center:

Jack, 17, drank a lot. Several older brothers and sisters drank. Jack recalls that the first day he walked into the high school, several teachers looked at him, and "didn't look happy to see me." Jack says one of the teachers told him, "Oh, yes, we know your family." Jack performed to their expectations. He continued to drink. After several major problems, he was kicked out of the high school. Some time later, he heard about an alternative school. He enrolled, felt accepted immediately, and reports, "Now I'm doing really well . . . learning a lot and getting good grades."[38]

It appears from these two reports that the alternative programs and centers—both public and private—are better able to meet the needs of the students who select them than their previous, assigned high schools. This is not surprising, given that most alternative schools are guided by a philosophy of providing nurturing learning environments that meet the needs of the students enrolled.

Still, these two programs and their reported successes do little to further the free-market philosophy of education. For instance, the reports cite no evidence that the Graduation Incentives and the Learning Centers programs have had any real impact on the school districts in the state. Unlike the Postsecondary Options plan, which supposedly spurred several school districts to provide more advanced-placement courses in an effort to dissuade high-achieving students from attending colleges and universities during their junior and senior years, these more recent programs, which attract a demographically different type of student, do not threaten high schools in quite the same way. To date, no evidence suggests that districts are creating new programs to retain academically unsuccessful students drawn to the Graduation Incentives or the Learning Centers program. Districts are not competing for them and their state education dollars.

Paradoxically, the very absence of the competitive free-market philosophy as a driving force behind these programs might explain why other states have not hurried to duplicate them. At a time when so much of our national and state educational policy-making is driven by competitiveness, a choice program that does not "force" schools to scramble for "customers" is less appealing. California, Oregon, and Washington all provide choice programs for students who are not succeeding in traditional schools, but these plans predate the Minnesota legislation. Washington established eight "educational clinics" for potential dropouts in 1978. Six are run by nonprofit agencies and the other two are for-profit clinics. Similarly, California provides funds to help school districts institute alternative programs and to support private nonsectarian "educational clinics" for potential dropouts not served by the districts. And Oregon allows unsuccessful high school students to enroll in state-approved private nonsectarian schools.[39] At the local level, many large urban school districts contract with private, nonprofit agencies to work with students not succeeding in regular schools.

Programs like the Graduation Incentives and Learning Centers may be less popular politically because they are geared toward students who, in the educational marketplace, are least competitive and have the fewest market resources. But as the research on alternative schools demonstrates, when students are given access to educators who respond to their individual needs, wonderful things can happen. And although these Minnesota programs are among the few recent statewide school choice programs not driven by a competitive ideology, they may prove to be the most successful in terms of actual student success.

OPEN ENROLLMENT

Despite these three extensive choice policies, Minnesota's K-12 Enrollment Options program—known as the Open Enrollment plan—remains far and away the best-known and the most emulated program. Adopted in 1987, this statewide choice policy allows students in any grade to transfer from one school district to another and to take their state per-pupil education dollars along.

Like the Postsecondary Options plan, the Open Enrollment plan is designed to offer individual families optimal choice in education and induce school districts to improve their educational offerings and compete for students. But like Postsecondary Options and other programs driven by the goal of greater competitiveness, Open Enrollment best serves the students and school districts that have the competitive edge.

In 1987, the first year of the program, participation on the part of school districts—both to allow resident students to transfer elsewhere and to accept incoming students—was voluntary. The legislation called for gradual expansion of the program to require all school districts to permit their resident students to transfer to the district of their choice. Thus, school districts of more than 1,000 students were required to participate beginning in the 1989–90 school year, and all districts were required to sign on by the 1990–91 school year. The number of students participating in the Open Enrollment plan grew quickly, from 140 students in the initial 1987–88 school year to 3,200 in 1989–90. By the 1992–93 school year, a total of 13,000 Minnesota students used the law to attend a school outside their district of residence. Despite this growth in numbers, the 1992–93 total represents only 1.8 percent of the state's student population.[40]

School districts now maintain the right, however, to decide when a nonresident student can transfer into one of their schools. But these decisions are to be made only on the basis of "capacity limits" or desegregation regulations. Districts are prohibited under the law from using any information regarding a student's previous academic achievement or disciplinary record in making an admissions decision. If the number of applicants to a particular district exceeds available space, districts use a lottery system to decide who will be allowed to transfer.[41] The desegregation regulations of the plan stipulate that students may not transfer from a district in which they are a racial minority into a district in which their racial or ethnic group is in the majority. For instance, a white student who lives within an urban, predominantly African-American and Hispanic school district cannot use the Open Enrollment plan to transfer to a predominantly white suburban school. Still, in St. Paul, where 58 percent of the students are white, 85 percent of the 308 students using Open Enrollment to transfer to whiter, suburban districts were white. Thus, although white students are not leaving a predominantly nonwhite district, their departure may soon create one.

As with the other statewide choice programs in Minnesota, the state does not provide transportation for students to get to the receiving school district, although, as with the Postsecondary Options program, stipends are available for students from low-income families. (Yet, as mentioned earlier, few low-income families have applied for transportation reimbursements, and only $11,600 of the $50,000 allocated for transportation reimbursements for both Postsecondary Options and Open Enrollment plans was spent during the 1990–91 school year.) Generally, though, if the transferring student can get to the boundaries of the receiving district, a district bus will transport him or her to school. Under a new provision in the legislation, school districts are also allowed to send buses into other districts to pick up transfer students. According to the Minnesota Department of Education, at least 71 school districts in the state send buses across their boundaries to transport more than 500 transfer students.

A small 1988 Minnesota Department of Education study of the program conducted during the first two years—when participation on the part of smaller school districts was voluntary—found that students involved in the program were "highly satisfied" with their new school. A survey of more than 100 parents of participating students in these first years revealed the main reasons why they chose another school district for their children: 44 percent cited curricular or academic reasons; 26 percent said location (i.e., the new school was closer to home, work, or day care); 23 percent stated better facilities and greater options; and 21 percent cited "social" or "psychological" reasons. This initial study also found that 90 percent of the students leaving their resident district were white, roughly the same percentage of students in the state who are white.[42] A 1992 study by Policy Studies Associates funded by the federal government found that 11 percent of the nearly 1,400 parents surveyed said the most important reason for transferring their son or daughter to a different district under Open Enrollment was the academic reputation of the new school. Another 9 percent cited educational services that were not available at the student's previous school, and 8 percent cited the learning climate of the new school. Still, 9 percent of these parents said that the new school's closeness to home was the most important reason for the transfer, 6 percent cited closeness to their job, and 4 percent said the most important reason was that child care was available before or after school.[43] According to the Carnegie report, however, school administrators in Minnesota assert that geography and convenience are, in fact, the overriding reasons for most transfers.[44]

Despite the lack of data on the progress and overall impact of Minnesota's Open Enrollment plan, the program has its fair share of critics, advocates, and healthy debate. One of the principal concerns of those who find fault is that smaller, more rural school districts will eventually be swallowed up by larger, neighboring districts. These critics see Open Enrollment as a disguised method of continuing school district consolidation, an understandable concern in a state that once had 8,000 school districts and now has fewer than 450.[45] Available data from state education officials suggest that the majority of students who have transferred through the Open Enrollment plan have moved from small to large school districts or from "unhealthy" to "healthy" districts and not the other way around. "Unhealthy districts" were those that were small, poor, shared grades with another district, were losing enrollment, or had teachers with less training. In the 1989–90 school year, before districts with fewer than 1,000 students were required to participate, nearly all of the districts that lost more than 4 percent of their enrollment had fewer than 300 students.[46]

What angers many opponents of the program is that it sets up smaller, less-wealthy districts for a competition they cannot possibly win because they lack the resources, facilities, and athletic teams to lure students from miles away. As the Carnegie report on school choice points out, statewide choice plans such as Open Enrollment tend to widen the gap between rich and poor districts. The report states that while these plans are built on a marketplace model, policymakers often overlook the fact that schools vary greatly in their capacity to compete because local resources differ dramatically from one district to another. In Minnesota, for instance, the difference in per-pupil expenditures between the lowest- and highest-spending districts is almost $7,000. "Clearly, when lower-spending districts are forced to vie with wealthier ones for students and dollars, they are placed in a bidding war they cannot win."[47] According to Judith Pearson, "healthy" districts also have healthy athletic programs, which lure students who want to play on winning teams. She said, furthermore, that these healthy school districts recruit student athletes—hockey players, in particular—from other districts. In one of the school districts neighboring the Mountain Irons Buhl district, where Pearson works, the high school hockey coach also serves as a part-time public relations representative and actively recruits students to his school. This particular district's P.R. campaign includes advertising on the paper bags of the region's only McDonald's.

Pearson and other critics argue that as students flee small districts to play on a better hockey team or for other nonacademic reasons, taking their $4,000 each in state education dollars with them, they abandon the remaining students—students who do not play hockey, or have a car, or whatever—in a district in even worse financial shape than before. Pearson said that districts suffering a loss of students and revenue in the first round of choice enter a downward spiral—the revenue losses force cuts in programs that prompt more students to leave, causing further cuts, and so on.[48] "It's an elitist plan," said Pearson. "The districts that start off losing students can't make a comeback. You can't add the programs that you need because you are too busy cutting the budget."

Although there is little data on exactly which students are participating in the Open Enrollment program in Minnesota or why they participate, the 1992 Policy Studies Associates report suggests that, like the Postsecondary Enrollment Options program, Open Enrollment tends to serve a higher-income, better-educated clientele. The study found that 64 percent of the students transferring to new school districts under this plan were from families with annual incomes greater than $30,000; 39 percent came from families with incomes greater than $40,000 a year. The report states that the authors lack the necessary 1990 census data to calculate the median family income in Minnesota, but they estimate that it is higher than the national median of approximately $29,000 a year.

The Policy Studies Associates researchers also found that the education levels of parents of students participating in Open Enrollment were unusually high. They note that while only 17 percent of Minnesota's adult population has completed four or more years of college, 36.4 percent of fathers and 31.5 percent of mothers of Open Enrollment participants had done so.[49]

Furthermore, opponents such as Pearson note that because it is often the students of the most involved parents who are the first to leave a financially strapped district for greener pastures, the sending district loses not only some of its highest-achieving students but also some of its strongest parent advocates of local tax initiatives to support public education. Meanwhile, when students transfer out of their local school district, neither they nor their parents have any political power in the new district. Parents cannot vote for the school board members who make the educational decisions that affect their children.[50]

On the other hand, supporters of the Open Enrollment plan can recite a litany of success stories: students whose lives were turned around when they transferred to a new district because they required a smaller, more personal educational setting, or needed to get away from peers who had become a bad influence. Nathan and Jennings write about 18-year-old Chris, who had never been particularly successful in school:

"I liked to hang around with my friends and party, but I didn't go to class much. My high school was too big, I just didn't like it." Then a friend told Chris about another, smaller school outside his district, about ten miles away. Chris recently wrote that without the law allowing him to attend this school, "I probably would not graduate. Choice not only gave me a chance to personalize my education, but it also gave me the confidence that I can make something of myself and control my destiny."[51]

The federally funded study of Minnesota's Open Enrollment plan by Policy Studies Associates reports changes experienced by students since transferring to new schools. The study found that 63 percent of the 920 participating students who responded to the survey said that their confidence in their own abilities had improved since they transferred. More than 50 percent said that their academic performance had improved, and 43 percent stated that they had higher educational aspirations. In terms of less academic and more socially oriented effects, 37 percent of these students said their participation in athletics had increased since their transfer, and 35 percent cited increased participation in extracurricular activities. Similarly, 52 percent said that their relationships with friends had improved in their new schools.[52]

Advocates also note that an unknown number of small, rural districts have responded to the competition by creating new magnet schools to attract students from larger school districts. In 1989, for instance, the tiny rural Cyrus School District turned its only elementary school into a math/science/technology school. Using the proceeds from parent-run bake and rummage sales, the school managed to purchase enough computers to have one for every three students. The curriculum includes measuring simulated earthquakes on computers and building computer-controlled Lego cars. The school markets its programs with brochures available in banks and offices inside and outside the school district boundaries. Students and the school mascot, a plywood robot named Dr. Megabyte, travel to nearby festivals and parades.[53]

But the Policy Studies Associates report paints a more dismal picture of the impact of Open Enrollment on educational programs and reforms throughout the state. For instance, of the 327 school administrators responding to a survey on the effects of the program, 89 percent stated that the Open Enrollment plan had no impact on the diversity of the teaching styles within their schools, 80 percent said the program had no impact on instructional innovation, and 78 percent cited no impact on teacher accountability. When asked about the potential long-term effect of the program, 61 percent of the administrators said it would probably not lead to new and innovative instructional strategies. The administrators also saw an impact on school finances—22 percent cited a negative impact and 14 percent saw a positive one.[54]

Individual students and schools are no doubt benefiting from the Open Enrollment plan, but it is still unclear—and may be for quite some time—whether the plan advances broader social goals, such as providing all students with equal access to viable educational offerings. As in the case of many competitive programs, the Open Enrollment plan could in fact lead to a situation in which the rich get richer. In other words, school districts with the resources (or parents willing to raise them) to provide outstanding services are reaping the most state money from the plan. The less popular districts—and the students who remain in them—are suffering.

Perhaps the strongest endorsement of Minnesota's Open Enrollment plan comes from the nine states that have enacted similar between-district transfer programs since 1987. Arkansas, California, Idaho, Iowa, Massachusetts, Nebraska, Ohio, Utah, and Washington all legislated Open Enrollment plans within six years of the creation of Minnesota's plan. But many of the problems and concerns raised in Minnesota have also surfaced in other states. In Iowa, only about one-third of the parents surveyed whose children participated in the Open Enrollment plan cited educational benefits or academic quality as their primary reason for exercising choice.[55] And a *New York Times* article describing the impact of Open Enrollment on the Des Moines school district reported that the city's white and affluent students were leaving the district to transfer to predominantly white suburban schools in such alarming numbers that the Des Moines school board attempted to bar any additional transfers by white students. In the first two years of the program, 402 of the 413 students who wanted to transfer to suburban districts through the Open Enrollment plan were white. While the parents of the white students who were hoping to transfer to the wealthier suburbs deny that their decisions were racially motivated, the school board argued that transfers would greatly accelerate white flight out of the 20-percent-minority-student urban district and that the white students would be taking much-needed state funding with them.[56]

But of all the statewide school choice plans, the original Massachusetts program has proven to be the most destructive. Unlike other Open Enrollment plans, Massachusetts permitted receiving districts to charge the sending district tuition equal to their own total per-pupil cost. Thus, sending districts were forced to pay receiving districts more than the equivalent of that student's per-pupil state aid. Some districts ended up owing more to receiving districts than their total district allocation of state aid.[57] For instance, in 1991–92, the first year of the Massachusetts program, 135 students from the tax-poor city of Brockton transferred to the wealthy suburban neighborhood of Avon. The Brockton schools, which spend an average of less than $5,000 a year per pupil, were forced to pay Avon $10,239—that district's per-pupil cost—for each student who transferred. The program drove Brockton into state receivership.[58]

Paul H. Gordon, executive director of the Massachusetts Association of School Committees, stated in *Education Week* that the funding mechanism for the Open Enrollment plan was "an absolute mess." He added that many districts had voted not to participate in the plan as receiving schools because "they reject the method of funding and feel that, even if they gain by it financially, they morally don't want to be responsible for the sending school districts losing that kind of money."[59] One Republican state representative who led an effort to repeal the law stated: "In Massachusetts, we really perverted the notion of what choice was all about. . . . It was a rob-Peter-to-pay-Paul scenario. Communities were making decisions purely for economic reasons and not for educational reasons."[60] In 1992 the Massachusetts legislature repealed sections of the law in an effort to ease the negative impact of the program. First, the lawmakers appropriated $2.7 million in one-time aid for districts such as Brockton that had lost a great deal of funding to wealthier districts. Second, they capped the amount of money a receiving district can take from a sending district at $5,000. In addition, sending districts are reimbursed 75 percent of their losses—the difference between their per-pupil costs and the $5,000 or less they must pay a receiving district—by the state. The plan also mandated that a parent information system be established by the state secretary of education. The lawmakers failed, however, to approve a transportation subsidy to reimburse transportation costs incurred by all students.[61]

Despite the obvious access and equity issues that have not been addressed by states with open enrollment plans, legislators in several other states are debating the feasibility of such plans.

CHARTER SCHOOLS

The most recent school choice legislation passed in Minnesota, the Charter Schools Act of 1991, aims to free educators from burdensome state and local regulations so that they can more directly cater to the needs of the students they serve. The key educational reform ideas of the late 1980s and early 1990s—"school-site management" and "teacher professionalism"—are embodied in this legislation. According to Ted Kolderie of St. Paul's Center for Policy Studies, a central idea is that the charter school should be a "discrete entity," apart from the regular public schools.[62]

Under the Minnesota act, one or more state-licensed teachers can design a school based on an educational theme or philosophy and request a charter to create it from a local school board. Furthermore, other government agencies, including a city council or the board of a public university, can become the charter school's sponsor. If the charter is granted, the educators are allowed to operate their schools fairly independently, with wide latitude in hiring teachers and designing curricula. Kolderie points out that while the law stipulates that the first approval for a charter must come from "a school board," it need not be the board of the district in which the teachers work or the board of the district in which their proposed school would be located.

The designers of the charter school and the sponsor, or granting agency, draft a "contract" of sorts that sets forth the specifics: composition of the school program, expected student performance, and the duration of the charter. A school could offer a specialized curriculum or method of instruction. It could cater to students of a particular age or those with special needs, including students who are at risk of failure or those with learning disabilities.

Despite the relative autonomy from state and local agencies and mandated curricula, charter schools are essentially public schools. They receive funding from the government, and they are not allowed to charge tuition. They must admit all students who apply or at least give everyone who seeks admission an equal chance through the use of a lottery system. "No picking and choosing 'nice kids'," writes Kolderie. "And no elite academies—academic or athletic."[63] Charter schools must also observe the same antidiscrimination policies that apply to all public schools, and they must meet basic health and safety codes. Charter schools cannot provide religious instruction or maintain a religious character.

The funding formula for charter schools is fairly straightforward. The money comes from the state and is essentially funneled through the local school district or whichever district grants the charter. The schools receive a per-pupil allotment equivalent to the statewide average for total per-pupil funding, which includes averages for federal, state, and local resources, but this total per-pupil amount is paid for out of the charter-granting district's state foundation aid. In addition, charter schools are eligible for categorical aid and for special state and federal grants. The Minnesota Charter Schools Act also exempts the charter-granting agency from any liability for acts involving the school, which must buy its own liability insurance to cover lawsuits over accidents that occur on its campus.[64]

At present, transportation is still not guaranteed for students who wish to attend charter schools, and this is one area of the legislation where more attention should be paid. As it stands, students attending charter schools have the same transportation options as students attending other schools of choice. Thus, if a charter school is able and willing to send buses to outlying areas or other districts, it can do so under Minnesota law. Still, the responsibility to get to a school of choice rests on the student.

Because the charter schools legislation was passed in the summer of 1991, the schools that were granted the first charters did not open their doors until the fall of 1992. Only a handful of charters were granted in the first year. This is, therefore, the least scrutinized of all the Minnesota statewide choice programs. Despite the absence of any track record, charter school legislation has become law in California, Colorado, Georgia, Massachusetts, and New Mexico, and has been introduced in Alaska, Arizona, Connecticut, Florida, Michigan, New Jersey, Oregon, Pennsylvania, Tennessee, Vermont, and Wisconsin.[65]

The California charter schools act was passed in September 1992. The legislation, which authorizes the creation of 100 charter schools statewide, went into effect in January 1993. The California charter school legislation differs from the Minnesota plan in a few important ways. First, the scope of the plan is much greater—100 charter schools in California as opposed to only 8 in Minnesota. Second, California charter schools are allowed to adopt admissions requirements although they cannot discriminate against applicants on the basis of ethnicity, national origin, gender, or disability. The legislation prohibits residency requirements for admission, although schools can give preference to students who live in the district. No student will be required to attend a charter school, and districts must provide transportation to other schools if nearby students choose not to attend the charter schools. In California, only public schools can apply to become charter schools, whereas, in Minnesota, private schools can be granted charters. And finally, under the California statute, petitions for charter schools must be signed by no less than 10 percent of the teachers currently employed by the school district or by no less than 50 percent of the teachers currently employed at the school that is applying. All petitions must be approved by the local school board before being sent on to the state board of education.

According to Kolderie, who has followed Minnesota's program, district superintendents and local school boards often deny teachers charters to create new schools or dramatically reform existing ones in an effort to keep state money and jobs within the districts. He cites the example of a teacher in St. Cloud who wanted to create an elementary school that would provide students with a different approach to learning involving cooperative and self-directed learning videos, computers, and other technology. The local school board refused to grant the teacher a charter but offered to let her create the program within a regular district school. The teacher said no thank you.

The Minnesota State Board of Education must approve the charters after they have been granted at the local level as well as review appeals from teachers who have been denied charters from local boards. The state board does not always rule in favor of the teachers either. In April 1992 *Education Week* reported that the state board rejected a proposal for a charter school in the town of Rapidan because, it claimed, there was not enough support for the school and the proposal was "simply an attempt to prevent the small school from being closed." According to the article, a group of teachers and parents had hoped to turn the Rapidan Elementary School into a charter school with a "country" theme focusing on "agribusiness" after they had learned that the school district planned to close the school.[66]

Despite such failed attempts by educators to create thematic schools, Kolderie has noted that school boards are more willing to use the charter law to create schools for those students who have not succeeded in traditional settings. For example, an alternative school for at-risk youth in St. Paul was granted a charter, as were programs for deaf and hard-of-hearing students in Lake Forest and for non-college-bound students in Rockford. According to Peggy Hunter, enrollment options coordinator of the Minnesota Department of Education, school districts tend to be more willing to sponsor programs that are the least threatening to their regular schools. A similar pattern may be developing in southern California, where continuation schools and those serving low-income students appear, in the early stages of implementation of the charter schools legislation, to be moving quickly through the application process while more popular and prestigious schools are facing more obstacles.[67]

The charter schools concept is unusual because it promises to release teachers from the constraints that often prevent them from teaching effectively. Competition is not the central driving force behind this legislation, although school boards may feel threatened by charter schools because they do siphon students and resources from the regular schools. This may in part explain the political support for charter schools that serve at-risk students—the students for which few educators want to compete.

Equity issues will certainly arise as more charters are granted, especially if these new, independent entities are to become popular schools of choice. This does not seem likely given the unwillingness of boards to grant charters to popular or potentially popular schools. But the question of who leaves and who is left behind must always be addressed in discussions of school choice plans.

Perhaps the ideal solution to the problem of how to serve both the common good and the individual needs of students would be a charter for every school, so that each school would be an autonomous school of choice. Under these conditions, the role of the school board would be to assure that all parents had access to information about the various charter schools, and that all students had adequate transportation. Teachers could work as professionals; tax dollars would not be drained from one district to the next. And most important, all students would be able to attend a school of choice. To operate such a program in an equitable fashion, however, charter schools would not be allowed to have admissions criteria, as they are under the California legislation.

Furthermore, if a school district were able to create such a charter-school choice plan, it might also include a "diversity component" that would facilitate the creation of racially balanced student populations at each charter school. Much like a controlled choice plan, a charter-school choice plan in which every school is a school of choice could contain guidelines that would make it easier for parents to choose integrated schools.

STATEWIDE SCHOOL CHOICE PLANS—
HOW THEY MIGHT BE IMPROVED

Unfortunately, Minnesota's experiments with statewide choice programs raise more questions than they answer. But preliminary evidence and common sense suggest that when state education money follows students from one district or school to the next, the students who leave profit, while those who stay behind suffer. The win-lose situations set up by competitive choice plans do not serve the common good.

Advocates of statewide choice programs argue that when students leave a school district through the Postsecondary Options or the Open Enrollment program, the district will respond by becoming more competitive and offering students a higher-quality education to entice them to stay. The shortsightedness of this competition-begets-better-education philosophy becomes apparent, however, when students transfer from one district to another in order to play on a better hockey team or enjoy nicer facilities. In such instances, the districts abandoned by fleeing students become progressively less able to "compete" in the educational marketplace as class sizes increase and course offerings shrink.

Statewide school choice plans can lead to more evenly distributed benefits, however, when state aid is targeted for at-risk youths who are on the verge of dropping out or for a group of educators who are free to design charter schools within a system in which all students are guaranteed a choice—policies based primarily on the idea of the common good and the need for individual growth. Such programs should also provide transportation for all students and create parent information and counseling centers within each district (an important component that is sorely lacking in Minnesota and other states with statewide school choice plans). And if such plans were tied to efforts to equalize educational funding throughout a state—not solely to bring the wealthy districts down to funding levels of the poor districts, but rather to raise all districts up to match the per-pupil expenditures of the wealthiest districts—and to a movement toward more state funding and less local funding, the impact on the common good would be significant. While these programs are not "competitive" in free-market terms, each has the capacity to guarantee a much-needed safety net for students who currently lack access, information, or transportation to participate in an Open Enrollment plan.

The alternative schools would be staffed by educators who understand why some adolescents have more trouble succeeding in a traditional school environment. In a sense, statewide choice directed toward these students reduces competition because traditional high school educators often encourage the most at-risk students to seek out alternative programs.

In a charter-school choice plan in which all schools would be charter schools of choice, with all students able to choose and racial diversity a district goal, competition among schools could occur, but it would not be the central driving force behind the program. In fact, if the plan were to look much like a controlled choice program, the district would encourage educators to duplicate popular charter school programs in more than one school and thereby better guarantee that all students and parents got their first choice of schools. This, of course, would greatly minimize the degree of competition among schools.

Although the verdict is still not in on the effectiveness of the Postsecondary Options program and the Open Enrollment plan, the fact that they are both guided primarily by the third educational goal—to train a competitive work force via a competitive school system—leads me to believe that they will likely serve some of the students some of the time. If that is all we, as members of a democratic society, demand from our schools, these programs will suffice, especially since they are fairly inexpensive and require little monitoring. But if we believe that the first and second educational goals—education for the common good and for individual growth and fulfillment—are necessary prerequisites for the creation of a well-educated work force, we might want to push our state governments to go beyond these quick-fix choice plans of the 1990s.

T he most important distinction to be made between proposals for school choice programs is whether or not they include private schools. Choice plans that go beyond the public schools and offer parents either tax credits or tuition vouchers to pay for private education cross a once well-defined boundary between the public and private spheres—between institutions governed by appointed boards and those governed by elected officials, between institutions with admissions criteria and religious or moral missions and those designed to serve all. These contrasts between public and private schools stand at the heart of the multifaceted debates over the "private-school choice programs" that allow parents to spend public money at private schools— whether they are fair, ethical, constitutional, or educationally sound.

Although only a handful of private-school choice plans exist, tuition voucher plans have rapidly gained political support in the last few years. Since April 1991, two federal voucher programs have been proposed, and at least 14 state legislatures have debated statewide school choice bills that would include private schools. Furthermore, a 1992 Gallup poll commissioned by the National Catholic Education Association concluded that seven out of ten Americans support the idea of a "voucher" system described therein as a government allotment of "a certain amount of money for each child" that can be redeemed at any public, parochial, or private school.[1] Only 50 percent of Americans had favored tuition voucher plans in a 1991 Gallup poll; the percentage of people in favor of vouchers has in fact increased steadily since the early 1980s.[2]

Still, such opinion polls can be misleading, given that private-school choice plans, and voucher programs in particular, come in several shapes and sizes. Taking the money-follows-children philosophy of the statewide choice plans one step further, private-school choice plans give parents some of the public money that would normally go toward educating their children in the public schools and allow them to spend it at any private school that accepts their children. Yet, beyond this general definition, proposals for voucher-type programs differ dramatically. Some allow parents to spend vouchers only at nonsectarian private schools; some are aimed specifically at low-income families and provide vouchers only to parents who fall below a certain income level; others place restrictions on voucher-redeeming private schools in terms of the amount of tuition that can be charged or admissions criteria; still others call for no regulation or restrictions whatsoever.

The diversity of voucher-type proposals reflects the wide range of political views and educational goals among those who support private-school choice plans. In recent years, conservative businessmen and policymakers who see vouchers as a way of infusing competition and market discipline into a "sluggish" public education system have become key supporters of the larger private-school choice movement. While these economics-minded voucher advocates cite several reasons for their support of private-school choice, including the desire to give poor parents the same educational options that the rich and middle-class have had for years, the main objective is clearly to force public education to compete with the private sector. In their view, such competition will make our public education system more accountable and—they hope—less expensive. The total deregulation they advocate would give every child the same voucher amount, free all schools from government control, and let the marketplace serve the educational needs of the society.

But the coalition of private-school choice supporters also includes civil libertarians who are more focused on the "equalization" function of vouchers—one that would give poor parents educational options typically limited to the wealthy. These advocates—who believe that the equalization of educational resources will serve the common good and free individual parents to seek the best education for their children, and that vouchers are one way to achieve these goals—are more likely to call for legislation that provides vouchers only to poor families or provides low-income parents with supplemental payments.

Many religious leaders and educators, particularly Catholic and fundamentalist Christians, also strongly support vouchers and private-school choice. Catholic voucher advocates point out that Catholic schools have successfully served low-income students in the past and warn that many urban Catholic schools, now struggling financially, will be forced to close if their constituents do not receive government support. Fundamentalist Christian leaders and educators, repulsed by the "secular humanism" of public schools, argue that parents have the right to spend their tax dollars on schools that impart their religious doctrine to their children—a Lockean liberal point of view. Thus, the goals and purposes of those who espouse private-school choice plans, although varied, frequently overlap. Yet, as this chapter will reveal, in the last eight years or so, the first group, the market-model voucher advocates, has dominated the policy debate on school choice, plugging into the arguments of other voucher advocates at the appropriate time and place.

Although many important issues need to be deliberated whenever a specific voucher program is proposed, many of these issues fall under one of three broad themes:

1. **Public versus Private Schools**—the critical differences in the missions, governance, quality, and effectiveness of public and private schools.
2. **Resource and Equity Issues**—the question of how public—federal, state, or local—education money will be redistributed under voucher or tax credit plans and how that redistribution

varies depending on the size and scope of a private-school choice plan.

3. **Constitutional Issues**—the church-state debate, reflecting concern over the use of public money for religious schools.

Most of the church-state debate has taken place at the federal level because arguments hinge on recent U.S. Supreme Court rulings and differing interpretations of the U.S. Constitution. The resource and equity battles concerning redistribution of educational funding tend to be more heated at state and local levels because, on average, approximately 92 percent of educational funding originates there. The public-versus-private-school debate occurs at every level and provides the philosophical framework for all related discussions.

This chapter, then, covers the public-private school debate and examines resource and equity issues within existing and proposed tuition voucher legislation. Chapter 6 examines political and constitutional barriers to tuition voucher programs.

PUBLIC VERSUS PRIVATE SCHOOLS— DIFFERENT MISSIONS, DIFFERENT OUTCOMES

Before the establishment of locally controlled public schools in the second half of the 19th century, a wide range of "private" and quasi-public schools served students of different classes, religions, races, and genders. At that time the line between "public" and "private" education was not distinct—state governments and cities provided public funds for many private schools, including religious schools, and parents of children in so-called public schools were often asked to pay supplemental tuition. According to historians David Tyack and Elizabeth Hansot, "Americans thought education a worthy cause, but they did not have united opinions about who should control or pay for it."[3]

In the mid-19th century, locally governed and financed common schools were founded in Massachusetts and other north-eastern states. These developed into a system of free, universal public education, followed by passage of the state compulsory attendance laws. By 1900 more than 90 percent of the nation's elementary and secondary schools were public.[4] The growth of tax-supported public education systems created a clear distinction between government and nongovernment schools and contributed to widespread political support for public education.

Throughout much of the 20th century, public and private schools were viewed as dissimilar institutions guided by different missions and serving separate purposes, with public education regarded as serving the larger good. David Tyack notes that free public education has long been seen as "a benefit like the air in which all participate and from which all may potentially benefit."[5]

Similarly, Henry Levin, an educational economist, writes that although public schools bestow many "private benefits," including individual earnings, trainability, health, and efficiency in consumption, "[t]here are few who would limit the purposes of schooling to only those aspects that enhance private lives. . . ."[6] He notes that the mission of public schools includes preparing children to support the important political, social, and economic institutions that comprise a democratic and capitalistic society as well as imparting a common set of values and knowledge to create citizens who can participate in that society. "To a large extent these requirements suggest that all students be exposed to a common educational experience that cannot be left to the vagaries of individual or family choice."[7]

On the other hand, the primary mission of private schools in this country is to provide parents and students with an "uncommon" education, distinct from that offered in the public schools. Private schools cultivate particular (as opposed to nonneutral) values and do so, in part, by selecting a student body based on such criteria as religion, prior achievement, class, race, and gender.[8] Peter W. Cookson, Jr., argues that a useful way of thinking about private schools is to conceptualize them as "moral communities," in which a group of people come together to share a vision of what constitutes a good school and a good life.[9]

Yet, this "shared vision" may be quite narrowly defined and

may, in fact, include principles that do not lend themselves to the creation of a good society—e.g., notions of moral, religious, racial, or gender superiority and a diminished sense of connectedness to the larger society. Furthermore, the "group" may share a vision that is intolerant and exclusive relative to society as a whole. After all, more than 21,500 of the nation's 26,836 private schools—81 percent—are religious institutions with missions that include the inculcation of beliefs of a particular denomination.

As Amy Gutmann points out, public schools are ideally held to certain educational standards, both curricular and noncurricular, deemed essential to the democracy. These standards include teaching a form of "democratic morality"—i.e., religious tolerance and mutual respect among races. Private schools, meanwhile, are not required to teach their students this common democratic morality.[10] In fact, the admissions criteria of private schools frequently send students messages that are antithetical to democratic morality. It would no doubt be difficult for a fundamentalist Christian school to preach religious tolerance and mutual respect for people of all races while excluding children on the basis of religion and race. Furthermore, as Anthony S. Bryk and Valerie E. Lee point out, students in Catholic high schools are more likely to be expelled for violating moral and religious norms than for academic reasons.[11] Public schools, on the other hand, cannot select or expel students based on their religious beliefs and values.

It is important, therefore, to question whether spending public funds on private schools actually benefits the common good. We must also question the fairness of a system in which wealthy and middle-class families are the only ones capable of placing their children in private "moral communities." Should we not equalize access to these institutions? And, if so, can a tuition voucher alone guarantee poor students equal access to private schools? These issues are discussed in the following section on resources and equity.

Another critical and overlapping distinction between public and private schools is their separate system of governance. Public schools are governed by democratically elected boards of education, which are theoretically responsible to their constituents, whether those constituents have children in the public schools or not. Although research and experience has taught us that school boards are often far less responsive to the needs of citizens—especially the poor—than they should be, the democratically run public education system holds greater promise for parental voice in school governance than does the private educational sector, particularly in religious schools.[12] As Michelle Fine, a social psychologist at the City University of New York, points out, in most parochial schools parents have neither choice of school (one school serves all children from a particular parish) nor the power to influence school policy. Fine adds that because most voucher plan proposals would allow private schools to maintain their admissions criteria, remain fairly free from government control, and still not be held accountable for the educational performance of the students they enroll, "voucher legislation enables not parents, but private and parochial schools to have choice—and dollars."[13]

Because public schools are governed by elected boards and designed to serve the general public, they are heavily regulated by federal, state, and local policies in the areas of curriculum, teacher certification, graduation requirements, discipline, testing, equal educational opportunities, and building standards. Private schools in most states must abide by minimal state requirements regarding health and safety standards for buildings, minimum hours of instruction per year, and child protection measures.[14]

Interestingly, many advocates of private-school choice plans argue that the most serious shortcoming of public education in this country is the degree to which it is overregulated and therefore stifled by bureaucratic control.[15] They seem to ignore the court cases and reams of evidence proving that, in the absence of any regulation whatsoever, schools and school systems continue to deny children of less politically powerful constituents—racial and linguistic minorities and the poor—access to a quality education. In fact, many private schools are deemed "good" precisely because they deny access to these same disfranchised students, who consistently score lower on standardized tests.

Private schools are frequently governed by appointed boards or trustees comprised of alumni or patrons with the most money or influence. Under a tuition voucher plan, these appointed trustees would be making critical decisions regarding how public voucher money would be spent at their schools, and yet the general public—those who pay the taxes that generate the vouchers—would have no say in how these officials are chosen. It sounds a bit like taxation without representation.

Beyond these significant public-private school distinctions of mission and governance, however, lies much diversity within both public and private sectors. This diversity makes any generalizations concerning quality and effectiveness of public versus private schools quite tenuous.

Public schools have traditionally received the majority of their funding from local revenue. This means that the country's 15,400 districts vary radically in terms of school size, class size, overall wealth, teacher qualifications, student composition, test scores, college-going rates, dropout rates, reform efforts, parent involvement, community involvement, facilities, discipline, traditions, and any other educational measure. The New York City Public School System, for instance, has nearly 1,000 schools serving more than 900,000 students, while the aforementioned rural Cyrus School District consists of one elementary school with 95 students. Suburban public school districts fall somewhere between in terms of size, but are usually distinct in terms of wealth of resources, small class sizes, sprawling modern campuses, and students whose families can finance their college education. John Witte, a political scientist at the University of Wisconsin-Madison, has challenged the view that American public education is a uniform monopoly or a simple, monolithic bureaucracy: "The institutional forms of American education are numerous and widely varied. . . . Schools are organized in different grade patterns, and it is very difficult to point to uniform patterns of curriculum, pedagogy and testing."[16]

The private school sector in this country also represents tremendous diversity, from inner-city Catholic schools serving low-income and minority children, to fundamentalist Christian academies, to Protestant and independent college preparatory schools that enroll mainly upper-middle-class and wealthy students—mainly WASP, although they have become much more ethnically diverse of late. According to the National Center for Education Statistics, 45 percent of the nation's 26,836 private schools are non-Catholic religious schools, which include main-stream Protestant, Jewish, and fundamentalist Christian schools. Catholic schools account for 36 percent of all private schools; and the remaining 19 percent are nonsectarian, independent schools. Because Catholic schools tend to be larger than the average private school, they enroll a disproportionate number —54 percent—of the 5.2 million non–public school students, and the percentage of non-Catholic children enrolled in these schools has increased from less than 5 percent in the 1970s to 12 percent today.[17]

In fact, the private school sector is so diverse that it is difficult to generalize about overall private school support for—or op-position to—tuition voucher plans. The reality is that those who run private schools are divided on the issue according to their differing beliefs about the role of private education and their fears that public money would bring greater government regu-lation. The division tends to run along denominational lines.

Private school educators from mainstream Protestant and Jew-ish schools as well as nonreligious, independent schools tend to be less enthusiastic about voucher proposals, which they say will drain public schools of needed government funding. "I would not want us to be seen as taking money out of the public coffer. I would not consider that to be for the public good," said J. Robert Shirley, headmaster of Heathwood Hall Episcopal School in Columbia, South Carolina.[18] When asked about tuition vouchers, Barbara Landis Chase, headmistress of the Bryn Mawr School, an independent all-girls school in Baltimore, replied, "There is a pretty strong misconception that all private school people are sitting around with bated breath waiting for this to happen." Chase, like other private school educators, fears that government money could bring government regulation.[19]

But Catholic and fundamentalist Christian educators tend to disagree. They say the public schools are failing, and the government would do better to allow parents to spend education dollars at the school of their choice.

Rev. Theodore Edward Clater, director of the Keystone Christian Education Association, a coalition of fundamentalist schools in Pennsylvania, said he strongly supported state legislation proposed in 1991 to give each school-age child $900 to attend private schools: "We believe that if there is any way to change education in America this is it—by infusing parents with responsibility and creativity. The one-size-fits-all public school system is not working."[20] The bill was killed in the Pennsylvania legislature.

Of course, the division among private school educators on the issue of vouchers has historical roots. Because American public schools were created and run by Protestants, most mainstream (as opposed to fundamentalist) Protestants—even those who send their children to private schools—have traditionally been strong supporters of public education; Catholics have commonly favored church-run schools. As the public schools became more diverse and less explicitly guided by Protestant philosophy, hundreds of fundamentalist Christian schools were founded for those who sought religious training and a more homogeneous student body than that found in the public schools. And Catholic schools, with their increasingly non-Catholic constituencies— particularly in inner-city neighborhoods—have come to see their mission as more broadly defined than simply serving the children of their parishioners.

Thus, the number of religious and private school organizations that support voucher plan proposals continues to grow. While the Catholic Conference and the National Catholic Education Association have remained staunch advocates of private-school choice programs, they are now joined by many fundamentalist Christian educators whose schools comprise one of the fastest-growing segments of American education.[21] Meanwhile, support from Catholic groups has intensified, in part because more than 100 Catholic schools—mostly in urban areas—have been forced to close in recent years.[22] The remaining urban Catholic schools now enroll many students from low-income families who cannot afford to pay tuition, and at the same time they are faced with a shrinking pool of low-cost teachers—i.e., nuns and priests. If poor parents had public money to spend on their schools, Catholic educators argue, more urban Catholic schools could remain open and poor families could send their children to the schools of their choice.

Not coincidentally, the private school educators who say they do not want to take public school resources tend to be those whose schools are financially stable and well endowed. These schools tend to serve higher-income families who do not necessarily need tuition vouchers in order to afford private education, and their tuition is usually much higher than the value of proposed tuition vouchers. Furthermore, because these schools have more applicants than they can accept, they believe tuition voucher programs will have very little impact on their enrollment. "We will have 1,200 to 1,400 applicants for 200 spaces in next year's seventh-grade class," said Thomas C. Hudnut, headmaster of the Harvard-Westlake School in Los Angeles, where 85 percent of parents are able to pay more than $10,000 in tuition. "As long as we are in a total seller's market because of the perceived condition of public education in Los Angeles, we are going to thrive with or without a voucher."[23] At such a school, tuition vouchers would be little more than a subsidy—a discount for wealthy families. Meanwhile, a voucher worth $2,500 or less would do little to help students of low-income families gain access to these most prestigious and expensive private schools.[24]

There is, however, evidence of a growing consensus among private school educators. For instance, early in 1992, 20 private and nonprofit religious and educational groups united to form the National Coalition for Improvement and Reform of American Education in support of the Bush administration's private-school choice proposal. This broad-based coalition includes the

National Association of Independent Schools, the Evangelical Lutheran Education Association, the Friends Council on Education, the National Association of Episcopal Schools, the National Society of Hebrew Day Schools, and the National Catholic Education Association.[25]

RESEARCH COMPARING PUBLIC AND PRIVATE SCHOOLS

Since the early 1980s, a body of educational research extolling the virtues of private schools has been published. Beginning with the well-publicized research on public versus private schools by James S. Coleman, Thomas Hoffer, and Sally Kilgore in 1982[26] and continuing into the 1990s with Bryk and Lee's influential work on Catholic high schools,[27] a number of books and articles have portrayed private schools as superior educational institutions because of their sense of community and their high expectations for students. All of this has taken place at a time when there has been little praise for public education and public institutions in general.[28]

The research on private education has been controversial and not without its share of critics, but all the literature boils down to one nagging question: Do private schools do a better job than public schools in educating similar students, or do they simply appear to because they enroll students who, for one reason or another, are predisposed to academic success? To my mind there is no adequate answer, in part because any "conclusion" could only be based on overgeneralizations about public and private schools. Furthermore, I believe that there are too many factors that distinguish parents and students who choose private, particularly religious, schools over public schools and even these distinctions may vary dramatically from one neighborhood or school district to the next. Still, a brief summary of some of the seminal work in this area may be helpful.

In terms of overall differences in enrollments, data from the National Center for Education Statistics reveal that private schools tend to be much smaller than public schools, with half of private schools enrolling fewer than 150 students. In terms of family income, only 6 percent of private school students qualify for free or reduced-price lunches while nearly a third of all public school students qualify.[29]

Racial diversity is far greater overall in public schools, but some analyses point to less school-by-school racial segregation in the private sector. Overall, the number of black students in private schools is about 5 percent, while nearly 20 percent of public school students are black.[30] Nearly half of all private schools have minority student enrollments of less than 5 percent, and only a small percentage of private schools have a student population that is more than 50 percent nonwhite, which means that the small African-American student population within private schools is fairly evenly distributed across various schools,[31] while in the public schools, school-by-school racial segregation remains high in northern and western metropolitan areas. Religious segregation is obviously much more prevalent in private schools.[32] But these student-body characteristics vary greatly within the private sector: Catholic school students are more likely overall to be segregated in terms of religion but less segregated by race, ethnicity, and social class than other private school students.[33]

Beyond issues of demographics, the primary question is one of effectiveness—are private schools better educational institutions? In 1981 and 1982, Coleman, Hoffer, and Kilgore released a report, several journal articles, and a book (*High School Achievement: Public, Catholic, and Private Schools Compared*) highlighting their analysis of a national data set known as "High School and Beyond." This data set contains survey responses and test scores from 58,000 students enrolled in 1,015 public, Catholic, and "other private" high schools.[34] The authors concluded that when they controlled for 17 background characteristics—including family income, race, parents' education, and family size—students in Catholic and other private schools had higher test scores than public school students in vocabulary and mathematics but not in reading.[35]

The authors also analyzed the data another way, attempting to assess test score gains between sophomore and senior years of high school. Although the sophomore and senior students taking the tests were not the same students tested at different points in their high school career but rather different cohorts of students, the researchers tried to compensate for this by conducting one analysis that eliminated students who were likely to drop out of school between their sophomore and senior years and another analysis that controlled for the 17 background characteristics.[36]

The authors drew the following conclusions:

(a) There is higher achievement and greater sophomore-senior growth in both the Catholic and other-private sectors than in the public sector in vocabulary and mathematics. The differences are substantial, on the order of magnitude of one grade level.

(b) Reading achievement in the other-private schools appears only slightly above that in the public schools for comparable students, but the sophomore-senior growth appears considerably greater. The reverse pattern appears for Catholic schools: greater sophomore achievement, but no more, and perhaps less, growth in reading achievement from sophomore to senior than in the public schools. These inconsistencies suggest only very small private-school effects in reading.[37]

The researchers also attempted to distinguish the factors that make private schools distinct from and more successful than public schools. They cited "discipline" and "student behavior" in particular[38] and concluded that "the greatest difference found in any aspect of school function between public and private schools was the degree of discipline and order in the schools."[39] And they argued that stricter disciplinary policies established at private schools lead to better-behaved students, lower absentee rates, and less truancy, fighting, and threatening of teachers. Such policies also mean that students complete more hours of homework per week.[40]

Immediately following the release of the Coleman, Hoffer, and Kilgore findings, a spate of articles appeared criticizing both the study—methodology and theoretical framework—and the authors' policy recommendations. James M. McPartland and Edward L. McDill charged that the conclusions and interpretations ignored the impact of social-class segregation and concentration of students from either high or low social-class backgrounds in public and private schools on both school climate and school effectiveness. They noted that:

> the social norms and expectations of teachers and students for academic behavior are the primary components of a school's learning environment, and these are strongly affected by the social background origins of the student enrollment. A school whose students are primarily from economically disadvantaged families and from neighborhoods with high levels of social problems will find it difficult to establish an environment of high academic expectations and strong learning motivations. In contrast, a school whose students are primarily middle and upper class, most of whom will go on to college, will find it much less difficult to establish an academically oriented climate. The psychological and social processes among both teachers and students created by a dominant core of advantaged students will typically produce a strong academic learning environment.[41]

McPartland and McDill pointed out that declining test scores and other signs of public school failure in the late 1970s were in part the result of the increased numbers of students from poor families who went on to high school, as well as middle-class flight out of urban areas during the 1960s and 1970s.[42] Thus, the concentration of poverty effects they cite contributed to lower student performance in many large urban districts and skews the overall public school sample.

Other papers that criticized the Coleman, Hoffer, and Kilgore findings cited problems with the tests administered to students in the national data set, the lack of longitudinal data to compare the same students over time,[43] and the statistical analysis employed by the authors.[44] Others focused on the issue of self-selection, stating that the parents who place their children in private schools—especially lower-income parents who must scrimp and save to do so—are also more likely to teach their children academic skills than demographically similar parents of public school students. These kinds of fundamental differences in parents and students from private schools cannot be factored out in a statistical analysis.[45]

In fact, another paper attacking the findings of Coleman, Hoffer, and Kilgore on more philosophical grounds states that the self-selection issue cannot be addressed as a problem of statistical control. "Controlling for the fact that parents choose private schools amounts to removing the differences in treatment between public and private schools."[46] Private schools, by their very nature, are voluntaristic, the authors contend, while public schools are forced to take all students, "including the disinterested and unmotivated." These differences in the ability and inability to select students have "important ramifications for constraining the way public and private schools operate."[47]

The public-private school debate sparked by the Coleman, Hoffer, and Kilgore study has yet to subside; in fact it has intensified with the release of more recent studies by these researchers and others. For instance, in 1987 Coleman and Hoffer published another book, *Public and Private High Schools: The Impact of Communities*, in which they argue that Catholic high schools form "functional" intergenerational communities strongly based within parishes. These functional communities, according to the authors, facilitate the interaction of students with many different adult members of the community and therefore create a form of social capital that furthers the goals of the school.[48]

This study was also controversial and highly criticized, particularly by researchers like Bryk and Lee, who note that Coleman and Hoffer provide no direct empirical evidence that such "social relations among schools and families actually characterize modern Catholic high schools."[49] Bryk and Lee also argue that the

Coleman and Hoffer conclusion is based on a false premise: "that most Catholic high schools are organized around individual parishes." They note that while this is correct for Catholic elementary schools, less than 20 percent of all Catholic high schools are parochial, and the majority are either private or diocesan, which means they draw students from highly diverse geographic areas. "This geographic separation actually mitigates against the intergenerational closure speculated by Coleman and Hoffer."[50]

Still, the idea that Catholic schools provide students with a distinctly different environment—one that may empower them academically—from that found in the public schools has gained much support in the last five years, even from some critics of Coleman and Hoffer. In fact, a growing number of educational researchers have concluded that poor and minority students enjoy more academic success in Catholic schools than do similar students in public schools. Richard F. Elmore, a professor of education at Harvard, was quoted in a 1991 *New York Times* article on Catholic schools as saying, "There's enough evidence that Catholic parochial schools, in particular, are doing a reasonably good job with kids who have at least some of the characteristics that public school people claim make kids difficult to teach."[51]

Researchers who study private schools cite several key ingredients of Catholic schools' success, including high expectations and a rigorous academic curriculum for all students, a great deal of personal attention from teachers who see their work as a mission, and an emphasis on shaping students' character. In a recent study on the effects of attending a Catholic high school, Bryk and Lee found that achievement gaps between white and black students and between students whose parents had very little education and those whose parents had advanced degrees were narrower in Catholic than in public high schools. Furthermore, the gaps grew smaller the longer the students attended Catholic schools.[52]

One of the critical factors contributing to this success of Catholic schools, according to Bryk and Lee, is the "core curriculum" required of all students, regardless of their background or educational plans. This means that all students in Catholic schools must take rigorous academic subjects, while many students—particularly poor and minority students—in public schools find themselves in vocational and remedial courses: "Although these differences result in part from the different types of students educated in public and Catholic high schools, there is also strong evidence of Catholic school policy effects."[53]

Other distinct and crucial factors in the success of Catholic schools cited by Bryk and Lee include the "communal organization" that characterizes Catholic high schools—it facilitates shared experiences between adults and students and extends the role of teachers beyond the classroom. Teachers, according to this study, "are mature adults whom students encounter in the hallways, [on] playing fields, in the school neighborhood and sometimes even in their homes."[54] Other "communal" components cited include the relatively small size of Catholic high schools, collegiality among teachers inside and outside the school, a set of shared beliefs about what students should learn and the proper norms of instruction, and a shared sense of how people should relate to one another.[55] Furthermore, the authors note that Catholic schools are basically autonomous and that "virtually all important decisions are made at individual school sites."[56] This decentralization, according to Bryk and Lee, is "predicated on a view about how personal dignity and human respect are advanced when work is organized around small communities where dialogue and collegiality may flourish."[57]

The authors wrap all of their observations into one all-encompassing concept of the Catholic school as a voluntary community—a place in which strong ties develop from a foundation of shared norms. Students who violate community norms must leave, and faculty who don't share the school's beliefs and commitments usually move on as well.[58]

Without questioning the extent to which many of these positive characteristics currently exist within some public schools or how they might be nurtured, particularly in a public-school choice plan that includes an emphasis on site-based management, Bryk and Lee conclude that policymakers could better serve the common good by helping to halt the closure of financially strapped Catholic schools, particularly those serving poor and minority neighborhoods. Bryk and Lee support the idea of tuition vouchers for parents who wish to send their children to Catholic schools, not because they see competition as the driving force behind educational improvement—in fact, they note that competitive market forces are not what cause Catholic schools to be good—but rather because they feel that giving more parents and students access to these voluntary communities is important and beneficial.[59]

Bryk and Lee provide a compelling argument, but they in failing to probe the likeness or potential likeness of Catholic school and some public schools of choice, they also fail to wrestle with the conflict between the idea of the common good in a religiously diverse society and policies that allow tax dollars to support voluntary Catholic schools, communities bound by a set of theology-based norms. They do, however, discuss issues of church and state, and conclude that we, as a society, place too much emphasis on this constitutional separation.

Another recent study, conducted by researchers at the Rand Corporation,[60] looked carefully at the similarities between three types of high schools—Catholic, special-purpose or magnet public schools, and regular zoned or neighborhood public schools—and found that educators in "focus schools" (Catholic schools and public magnets) concentrate more on student outcomes than educators in neighborhood schools, who are more concerned with delivering programs and following procedures.[61] The researchers reported that focus schools have "strong social contracts" that spell out the responsibilities of administration, students, and teachers and "establish the benefits that each derives from fulfilling the contract faithfully." The zoned schools, on the other hand, let students and staff define their own role in the school whenever possible.[62]

The Rand study points out several characteristics that Bryk

and Lee identified with Catholic high schools as also existing in "special-purpose" public schools of choice, including a challenging academic curriculum for all students and a strong commitment among faculty to teach students more than just subject-specific material—i.e., to mold student attitudes and values by emphasizing the "secular ethics of honesty, reliability, fairness, and respect for others."[63] They also found that focus schools—public or private—typically have a distinctive character and are more likely to be responsive and accountable to the members of their communities, including parents and students.[64]

"Key features of focus schools can be reproduced broadly in public schools," the authors conclude, "and the vast majority of public school students can profit from schools with those features."[65] This means the debate should not center on whether public or private schools are better, but rather on what policies enable public schools to take on some of the positive characteristics of private schools without excluding children on the basis of religion, gender, or ethnicity.

Consideration of private school characteristics that public schools might adopt should not, however, lead educators and policymakers to conclude that all private schools are good, and therefore deserve public money, or that all public schools are bad because they don't look and act "private" enough. Plenty of research and anecdotal information documents the existence of "bad" private schools, not to mention private proprietary schools that lure poor students eligible for government tuition loans and then fail to prepare them for any marketable trade. What is more important than pitting public and private schools against each other is recognizing the different missions and purposes they serve while always questioning what they can learn from each other. The argument over whether or not tuition vouchers for private schools are a good idea or sound educational policy should not be driven by overgeneralizations about the quality of two diverse educational sectors.

RESOURCE AND EQUITY ISSUES

Given the unlikelihood that the amount of public money allocated to education will increase dramatically in the near future, it is critical to understand how the total education pie will be sliced under a voucher plan— how much public money will be spent on children from poor, middle-class, and wealthy families, and to what degree and in what direction the distribution shifts with the move toward vouchers.

Like all other forms of school choice, tuition voucher programs take many forms, and the redistribution of public education dollars will vary dramatically according to the parameters of each plan. Once again, it is easy to see the ideology of the proponents of a particular voucher plan in the details of the proposal: Civil libertarians who favor vouchers as a way to make choice a reality for both rich and poor are more likely to propose either that only poor and lower-middle-class families should be provided with public funds for private schools or that lower-income families should receive larger vouchers than the wealthy.

On the other hand, voucher advocates who are driven mainly by the desire to make schools act more like small businesses— competing for customers and meeting the bottom line—tend to put forward plans that provide the same size voucher to every student and leave all to fend for themselves in the educational free market.

This is not to say that these two goals of free choice and school competition are mutually exclusive or that one who believes competition leads to better education does not want all families to have choice. On the contrary, such a voucher advocate might consider the two goals complementary: Competition cannot exist without consumer choice. But it is also true that voucher proponents who are primarily concerned with guaranteeing every family real choice will devise a different program than will those who subscribe to a trickle-down theory of educational improvement through increased competition.

DIFFERENT MODELS OF VOUCHER AND
PRIVATE-SCHOOL CHOICE PLANS

As early as the 18th century, philosophers such as Adam Smith, Thomas Paine, and John Stuart Mill argued that the fairest, most efficient method of funding education was for the government to give parents tuition money and let them spend it at whatever schools they chose. While such proposals were not exceedingly popular in this country during the 19th and early 20th centuries, in the late 1950s economist Milton Friedman began promoting the idea of tuition vouchers based on similar libertarian principles. Friedman received quite a bit of attention by claiming that public education's inefficiencies could be corrected through a competitive, free-market system in which all parents were given a set sum of public tuition money—equivalent to the per-pupil amount spent on children in their school district—and complete freedom of choice in selecting schools for their children.[66] Friedman wrote:

> Government could require a minimum level of schooling financed by giving parents vouchers redeemable for a specific maximum sum per child per year if spent on "approved" educational services. Parents would be free to spend this sum and any additional sum they themselves provided on purchasing educational services from an "approved" institution of their own choice. The educational services could be rendered by private enterprises operated for profit, or by non-profit institutions. The role of the government would be limited to insuring that the schools met certain minimum standards, such as the inclusion of a minimum common content in their programs, much as it now inspects restaurants to insure that they maintain minimum sanitary standards.[67]

What Friedman proposed then was a highly deregulated voucher plan by which wealthy parents could use vouchers as a discount for tuition at expensive private schools. Students from low-income families would not receive supplemental assistance to help them meet the cost of more expensive schools. The private schools would remain free to pick and choose among students based on any criteria, from student "ability" to religion to ideology. Friedman did not discuss how parents would receive reliable information about the various options, nor did he call for schools to provide transportation.[68]

The next well-known voucher advocate—Christopher Jencks—proposed a very different private-school choice plan guided by the goal of providing more equitable access to private schools. As noted earlier, Jencks developed a highly detailed blueprint for federally funded vouchers while serving as a consultant to the U.S. Office of Economic Opportunity during the late 1960s. Jencks's plan called for greater regulation of participating schools and was geared toward helping low-income students.[69]

The Jencks proposal, designed for elementary schools, would offer all parents a voucher equal to the cost of schooling in an area chosen for the voucher experiment. Supplementary federal funds would be available for poor children, and wealthy parents would not be allowed to "add on" personal funds to the voucher amount. Private schools would, therefore, have an extra financial incentive to admit students from economically disadvantaged backgrounds, and wealthy parents would not be able to use a $2,500 voucher as a "discount coupon" at a private school that charged more in tuition than the voucher amount.[70]

Jencks also insisted that participating schools meet the various requirements of the state and the local district. His proposal did not allow schools with certain philosophical or political orientations—or with discriminatory admissions policies—to redeem vouchers. Oversubscribed schools were to admit half of their students through a lottery.[71] Under the Jencks proposal, all participating students would be offered free transportation to and from their school of choice, and schools would be required to provide parents with detailed information about test scores, educational programs, teacher qualifications, and school facilities.[72]

In the early 1970s, efforts by the Office of Economic Opportunity and the National Institute of Education to launch a federally funded voucher demonstration project based on the Jencks plan fell far short of expectations. Because of strong opposition from the teachers' unions, only one district—the Alum Rock Unified School District in California—accepted the federal government's invitation to participate in the experiment.[73] And even in Alum Rock the voucher plan had to be scaled back considerably due to political opposition from the teacher's union: Private schools were not included in the Alum Rock plan, and the district could not fire teachers who failed to attract students to their classrooms.[74] Furthermore, as was mentioned earlier, the Alum Rock experiment was fairly unsuccessful, with many low-income, poorly educated parents opting not to choose new schools for their children or choosing schools based on location and convenience.

Despite the difficulties faced by the federal government in its efforts to launch a tuition voucher program and the extreme differences between Friedman and Jencks, with their radically different visions of what a voucher plan ought to look like, these two men ignited a new debate over the structure and funding of American education. Suddenly, the once-taboo idea that parents who send their children to private schools should receive greater support from the government—through a tax deduction, tax credit, or a voucher—was being discussed and entertained by policymakers at the federal and state levels.

In fact, proposals for federal income tax credits for private school parents have been brought before Congress on several occasions since 1969. Although these proposals have passed in the Senate numerous times—in 1969, 1970, 1971, 1976, 1977, and 1978—they have yet to pass in the House of Representatives. In 1978 the Packwood-Moynihan bill was finally approved in the House of Representatives—the House's only approval of a tax credit plan thus far—but not before the provision allowing credits for elementary and secondary schools was removed, limiting the scope of the bill to higher education.[75] The Reagan administration tried repeatedly to put through legislation for tuition tax credits for parents of children in private schools[76]—in 1982, 1983, and 1984—but in every case the legislation died in Congress.[77]

At the state level, various tax credits have been approved and challenged in court.

Many tuition voucher programs have also been proposed at the state level. In the late 1970s, John Coons and Stephen Sugarman, two California lawyers who specialize in school finance, proposed a constitutional initiative for a statewide program to give parents vouchers equivalent to 90 percent of the statewide per-pupil cost for each child. At that time, each voucher would have been worth about $2,000. Under the initiative, the state legislature would have been able to allocate larger vouchers for certain purposes, including serving handicapped and bilingual students, compensating for variations in local costs and funding, and encouraging racial integration.[78] The Coons and Sugarman initiative did not call for increased state regulation of private schools. But it did require participating schools to maintain nondiscriminatory admissions policies with regard to race and religion, but not gender. In cases where the number of applicants exceeded available places, the voucher-redeeming schools were to use a lottery system to select students.[79] The plan also mandated both pupil transportation and information services to familiarize parents with choice schools.[80]

The goals and philosophies behind the Coons and Sugarman proposal were spelled out in their 1978 book, *Education by Choice: The Case for Family Control*, in which they make a strong "equity" case for tuition vouchers by emphasizing the need for parental freedom in choosing the right school for their children, the economic inequity inherent in the current system of public education finance, and the potential of choice to lead to more meaningful and long-lasting racial integration.[81] But Coons and Sugarman failed to convince many California voters of the merits of their plan, and the initiative campaign fell far short of the needed half-million signatures to qualify for the ballot.[82]

RECENT HISTORY

By the mid-1980s, the optimism among proponents of tuition tax credit and voucher programs had waned as a result of these legislative defeats. In 1990, however, the release of *Politics, Markets, and America's Schools*, by John E. Chubb and Terry M. Moe, brought these issues back into the national debate with more support than ever. Using statistical analyses that are little understood by most policymakers or laymen, Chubb and Moe claim to have traced the link between school governance—democratic public schools versus autonomous private schools—and student achievement. They conclude that privately run schools are better organized and therefore facilitate greater student achievement among similar students. According to Chubb, of the Brookings Institution, and Moe, of Stanford University, these findings provide the much-needed empirical evidence confirming that the government should get out of the business of operating schools and simply provide all parents with the tax money to send their children to the school of their choice.[83]

People with no statistical training tended to accept this study as validating arguments for tuition vouchers. More qualified observers, however, found the study weak in design and analysis, and the findings and implications questionable at best. The authors employed follow-up data from the same national data base that Coleman, Hoffer, and Kilgore had used for their study on Catholic schools. Chubb and Moe examined actual test score gains for students between the 10th and 12th grades, then weighted the gain scores with a questionable statistical calculation that favors students who had high scores on the initial 10th-grade test.[84] The authors then placed the schools with the highest average test score gains in a group labeled "high performance" and those with the lowest 10th-to-12th-grade gains in a group called "low performance." The average schools in the middle were disregarded.[85]

Chubb and Moe attempted to demonstrate that the high-performance schools were better organized—and, more important, that the reason why they were better organized is because they were private "market-driven" schools instead of public "democratically controlled" schools. In fact, the "school organization" variable they constructed to demonstrate its effect on student achievement actually proved to have very little effect on student test score gains.[86]

Chubb and Moe's book was the first well-publicized call for tuition vouchers in several years, it came from researchers at respected institutions, and it appeared to be backed by a great deal of convincing statistical analysis—at least to the untrained eye. Before criticism of the study by other researchers had surfaced, voucher supporters immediately began to rally. President Bush surprised many observers when, midterm, he suddenly switched from being a supporter of public-school-only choice plans to being an advocate of tuition vouchers for private and parochial schools. The policy shift occurred in April 1991, when the President and his new Secretary of Education, Lamar Alexander, released an educational reform plan—"America 2000"— which called for the creation of national standards and national tests in five core subject areas, a system of privately funded "break the mold" schools, and federal grants for states and local school districts that were willing to experiment with private-school choice programs.

The central message from the Bush administration was educational reform through and for economic competitiveness:

> . . . Serious efforts at educational improvement are under way by most of our international competitors and trading partners. Yet while we spend as much per student as almost any country in the world, American students are at or near the back of the pack in international comparisons. If we don't make radical changes, that is where we are going to stay.[87]

"America 2000" was a reform plan propelled by a vision of education for a more competitive work force—with scant attention to any other goals. Thus, public schools, without any equalization of their highly inequitable funding, were to compete with one another and with private schools for clientele on the basis of national standards as measured by national tests. Private schools, which can select their students and remain free from government regulation designed to ensure that all children are well served, will no doubt come out ahead in such a competition.

Anyone closely following national educational policy debates in the late 1980s might have guessed that President Bush would inevitably support school choice plans that included private schools. Such a voucher plan fit too neatly into the larger political philosophy of the Reagan-Bush era—a laissez-faire style of government stressing the value of a deregulated, competitive free-market system in every sphere of social and economic policy and a major push to privatize everything from the U.S. Postal Service to public housing projects. Although this political change of heart by the President was not nearly as well publicized as his broken "read my lips, no new taxes" pledge, it was perhaps more devastating to those who believe in the importance of public education and broader educational goals.

But "America 2000" proved to be a weak catalyst for a federally funded voucher program. Both houses of Congress omitted private school choice from their education reform bills for 1992. The Senate, for instance, voted 56 to 38 against a voucher plan amendment to its 1992 education bill.[88] After the Senate vote, a House education bill was amended to omit a section allowing states and school districts to use federal grant money for private school tuition vouchers. By the end of the last session of the 102nd Congress, the final version of the congressional education reform bill which contained no funding for private-school choice plans died in the Senate after the House had passed the measure.[89] These recent developments prove that even in a conservative era rampant with the free-market ideology that fuels tuition voucher and tax credit proposals, the U.S. Congress remains opposed to legislation allowing parents to spend public funds on private school tuition.

In June 1992 President Bush proposed the "Federal Grants for State and Local 'G.I. Bills' for Children," a separate piece of private-school choice legislation. This proposal—an election-year ploy to keep the school choice issue alive and demonstrate the President's concern for low-income families—lacked the competitive tone of "America 2000." It offered to provide $1,000 vouchers to children in families with annual earnings below the national or state average of about $40,000,[90] thus "freeing" them from the public schools.

The proposal would have allowed parents to spend the voucher on any private school their children gained access to—religious or independent. Referring to the extremely popular G.I. Bill of Rights, which gave World War II veterans federal grants to continue their education, Mr. Bush said, "No one told the GIs they couldn't go to SMU or Notre Dame or Yeshiva or Harvard."[91] Although it went nowhere with Congress, Bush's second private-school choice plan was well received by Catholic educators and more conservative libertarian groups, including the Institute for Justice in Washington, D.C.—a legal advocacy organization that represents low-income families seeking tuition vouchers as remedies.[92]

At the state level, there have been ongoing battles over these issues since the late 1980s. According to the American Legislative Exchange Council (ALEC), a bipartisan organization of state lawmakers who advocate free-market principles, at least 14 state legislatures have considered tuition voucher bills since 1990. Although a Milwaukee program that allows low-income children to attend nonreligious schools is the only such plan to have passed thus far, Patricia A. Farnan, the director of education and empowerment policy for ALEC, predicts that it is only a matter of time before a state passes a voucher law that will include both private and parochial schools: "And when you see one go, you'll see four or five . . . right behind it."[93]

One of the most intense state legislative battles occurred in Pennsylvania—a state with a high percentage of children enrolled in private schools—at the end of 1991 when the state senate approved a school choice bill that would have given parents a $900 voucher for each child to spend at private or parochial schools. Voucher proponents launched a major effort—including a letter-writing campaign led by the state's powerful Catholic Conference and a coalition of citizen groups, fundamentalist educators, and business leaders known as Road to Educational Achievement through Choice (REACH)[94]—to get the legislation through an unsupportive state assembly. In response, an anti-voucher campaign was launched by the Pennsylvania teachers' union. Opponents predicted that the cost to the state in vouchers for just those families whose children were already attending private and parochial schools would exceed $340 million.[95] Opposition to the private-school choice section of the bill remained strong in the assembly, even though proponents of the measure agreed to add a means test to exclude all families with annual incomes above $75,000. Ultimately the assembly defeated the measure.[96]

Meanwhile, similar voucher legislation proposals were introduced in Alabama, Florida, Georgia, Idaho, Iowa, Louisiana, Maryland, South Carolina, and Tennessee during 1991–92, although these legislative efforts also failed.[97]

In a handful of other states, voucher advocates are now trying to get private-school choice programs onto statewide ballots by 1994. A group known as the Excellence Through Choice in Education League (EXCEL), comprised mostly of Los Angeles business leaders, launched an aggressive campaign in California to place their Parental Choice Initiative on the November 1992 ballot. The initiative came up a few thousand signatures short of qualifying, but EXCEL members succeeded in qualifying it for the June 1994 ballot. Then, in May 1993, California governor Pete Wilson called a special statewide election for November 2, 1993, which means California voters will decide the fate of the choice initiative seven months earlier than expected.

If passed, the California initiative will amend the state constitution to give parents at least 50 percent of the total amount of state and local public school funding per student at a given grade level, calculated on a statewide basis. Parents will be able to redeem this sum—approximately $2,600—at any voucher-redeeming private school. Parents of students enrolled in private schools at the time the initiative passes would be eligible to receive publicly financed vouchers or scholarships by the 1995–96 school year. There would be no supplemental vouchers for low-income or handicapped students, nor would there be any transportation to schools of choice. Also, there would not be a cap placed on the amount of tuition that voucher-redeeming schools could charge; thus, these state-funded vouchers would become coupons for many, allowing wealthy people $2,600 off the cost of exclusive and expensive private schools. The total cost to the state of providing vouchers to the 544,000 students currently enrolled in private schools would be about $1.4 billion, which would be siphoned off state funds for public schools.

A new brand of independent "public" schools could also opt to redeem tuition vouchers under the California plan. In order to participate in the plan and receive the tuition vouchers, these independent "public" schools would have to agree to operate autonomously from the local school district, thereby relinquishing their regular federal, state, and local funding. In return they would be allowed to set admissions standards and have complete control over the school's curriculum. If it passes, the Parental Choice Initiative will create a situation in which public money will follow students to schools that they choose and are chosen by.

Private-school choice proponents in Colorado were successful in getting a similar voucher initiative on the 1992 ballot but voters overwhelmingly rejected the proposal, 66.8 percent to 33.2 percent. The Colorado initiative would have given parents a voucher of approximately $2,500 each year to pay for tuition at private or parochial schools. The Colorado initiative did not contain vouchers for "independent public schools," as the California initiative does, but it would have allowed parents to use public funds to cover the cost of educating a child at home.[98]

In Oregon, voters defeated a tax credit initiative in 1990, but a group known as TEACH Oregon (Toward Educational Accountability and Choice) has drafted a new school choice initiative for the 1994 ballot. A similar citizen and business coalition in Michigan plans to propose a statewide ballot initiative for 1994 as well.[99]

For some reason, voucher advocates who fight for private-school choice programs that make the same amount of public money available to all families—rich and poor alike—seem to ignore the massive redistribution of public money that would occur under such plans. For instance, a state tuition voucher plan that gave every student $2,500 to spend on a public or private school of choice would immediately shift millions—billions in California—of state education dollars away from children of lower- and middle-income families, most of whom currently attend state-funded public schools, and into the pockets of many wealthy families that now pay private school tuition without any government assistance. This redistribution would occur whether or not students from poor families opted to attend a private school under the voucher plan. Either way, the state would spend a smaller percentage of its total education budget on the students from the low- and middle-income families than it does now, because it would have to give a significantly larger amount to families who currently send their children to private schools.

If tuition voucher programs are to be implemented, voters and taxpayers need to consider these issues, and ask whether or not they want public funds to subsidize the education of students from wealthy families who have already chosen to attend expensive private schools. Taxpayers should also consider the important issue of "taxation without representation," which will, by definition, occur under any program that gives tax dollars to privately run institutions. In other words, those who pay taxes so that parents can have vouchers to spend at private schools have no recourse should these private schools develop policies or practices that are offensive or exclusionary.

EXISTING VOUCHER PLANS

As noted earlier, the Wisconsin legislature passed a law permitting up to 1,000 children from low-income families in Milwaukee to spend their state per-pupil aid—about $2,745 for the 1992–93 school year—at the private nonsectarian school of their choice. The amount of the voucher is then deducted from the total budget of the Milwaukee Public Schools. Participation is limited to families whose income is within 175 percent of the federal poverty level—about $22,000 for a family of three—and to Milwaukee public school students who have not been enrolled in a private school for at least one year. Participating private nonreligious schools must be within the city limits, and they cannot draw more than 49 percent of their student body from the voucher plan. These schools cannot discriminate in their selection based on race, religion, gender, prior achievement, or prior behavioral records. They can, however, refuse to admit physically and mentally handicapped students on the basis of not having the facilities or resources to serve them. Either the receiving private schools or the parents must provide transportation, reimbursable by the state.[100] Participation is limited, for the time being, to 1 percent of the city's public school children.

In the 1990–91 school year, about 350 students and 7 of the 18 private nonsectarian schools in the city took part in the program. By the 1991–92 school year, the total number of students participating had grown to 562, many of whom were new to the program because the first-year "class" had an extremely high attrition rate. By the 1992–93 school year, the total number of accepted choice students was 632. Furthermore, only six of the original seven private schools participated in the program's second year, although five new private schools signed on for the 1992–93 school year. Due to limited participation in the program on the part of the 18 eligible private schools, the number of student applicants exceeded the number of students enrolled by 236 in 1990, 168 in 1991, and 357 in 1992.[101]

In his study of the first year of the program, John F. Witte, a political scientist at the University of Wisconsin-Madison, found that private school vouchers did not appear to cream off the highest-achieving public school students. Instead, he found, the choice program attracted students who had not been succeeding in the public schools and were probably more likely than average to have behavioral problems. These findings, it should be noted, are based on comparisons of the voucher students with the average Milwaukee public school students, not with other low-income students. About 78 percent of the students in this program came from families with incomes of less than $15,000 in 1989. Furthermore, in his study of the second year of the program, Witte found that the students who left the private schools after the first year to return to their public schools were higher achievers, with test scores significantly higher than students who continued in the program.

But in both the first- and second-year reports Witte found that the parents who opted for private schools under the voucher plan tended to be more involved in their children's education than average Milwaukee public school parents, and that their level of involvement increased when their children began attending private schools.[102]

Data from the second year of the program demonstrate that the choice parents have more years of education than Milwaukee public school parents in general and even more years of education compared with other low-income families with children in the public schools. For instance, 45 percent of the mothers of choice students, as opposed to 29 percent of the average Milwaukee public school mothers and 26 percent of other low-income mothers from the district, had "some years" of college education. In both years, Witte found that parent satisfaction with the private choice schools was significantly higher than their satisfaction with their former public school.[103]

Data on student achievement with the first year of the choice plan were inconclusive. According to Witte, the results were mixed: "As a group, the choice students went up somewhat in reading, but declined in math." Even when compared with a similar group of low-income students who remained in the Milwaukee public schools, the choice students surpassed the comparison group in reading only, and actually fell behind in math.[104] In the second year, math and reading test scores for children completing two years in the choice program were lower than the district average scores for Milwaukee public schools and lower than the scores of other low-income students who had remained in public schools. Witte argues that this fluctuation in achievement test scores for choice students was in part an effect of high attrition in the program and the fact that the high achievers were more likely to leave the program. At the end of the first school year, 1990–91, 47 percent of participating students left the program. In the second year, the attrition rate was 35 percent.

One private school—the Juanita Virgil Academy—closed its doors halfway through the first year of the voucher program, sending the 63 choice students back to their public schools. This particular school had offered a curriculum focusing on the culture and accomplishments of African and African-American people, and had, until it began participating in the voucher program, also offered a religious Muslim education. According to articles and reports, several things went wrong at this particular school. The first-year report on the Milwaukee program by Witte stated that parents at the Juanita Virgil Academy had complained about a shortage of books, overcrowded classrooms, dirty facilities, lack of discipline, and transportation problems.[105] A principal at another participating private school said that many of the parents who had sent their children to Juanita Virgil before the voucher program began were upset that the school had decided to discontinue the religious instruction in order to participate. In fact, the directors of the school decided to withdraw from the choice program so that they could reinstate religious training at the school. The state Department of Public Instruction granted the school's request, and several weeks later the school closed completely.[106]

Based upon two years of research on the Milwaukee program, Witte suggests that the state should require that participating private schools have a formal governance structure (such as a board of directors), make public an annual financial audit, and be required to meet the same "outcome" requirements as the public schools, including statewide tests, dropout reporting, and school report cards.[107]

The state's then superintendent of public instruction, Herbert

J. Grover, and other opponents of the plan (including the teachers' union and the Milwaukee chapter of the National Association for the Advancement of Colored People) continually criticize the program. Speaking at the Economic Policy Institute Conference on School Choice in October 1992, Grover said that the Milwaukee choice program is unfair to public schools because they are still required to meet state guidelines in several areas while the participating private schools they compete against are not. He noted, for instance, that at least two of these private schools have illegal levels of asbestos in their walls and ceilings. He also pointed out that private schools' ability to reject handicapped students places a larger financial burden on public schools at a time when they are losing state funding through the program. In addition, the private schools accepting choice students in Milwaukee pay their teachers far less than the public schools.

But the Milwaukee Private-School Parental Choice plan will continue; it has withstood court challenges and was ruled constitutional by the Wisconsin Supreme Court in March 1992. No further court challenges should be forthcoming, since no federal constitutional issue exists, due to the fact that only nonsectarian private schools can participate.[108] The more likely scenario is that the Milwaukee plan will be closely followed over the next couple of years and seen as a model to be expanded and replicated.

Another existing private-school choice plan worth mentioning is the decades-old tuition law in Vermont, a state in which some 80 small towns do not have their own public high schools. Students who live in these towns are able to choose a public school in another town or district, and the town in which they reside pays the full per-pupil cost. If the families choose a private school, the town pays the private school the average cost per pupil at a public high school in the state, and the parents must pay any remaining balance.[109] According to a report on this law by Susan Schacht:

> It isn't clear whether competition is more the rule or the exception in Vermont. State officials say schools are often too few and far

between to really fight for the same students. New schools don't
crop up easily amidst such a sparse population. The state doesn't
require towns or private schools to provide transportation, so
busing is scarce. . . . Students tend to go to the nearest school.[110]

In fact, Schacht notes that even when students have real choices
involving more than one school, "families don't always favor the
one with the strongest record on student achievement." According to a consultant to the state department of education,
some students may pick a school in a town with "the most familiar
way of life."[111]

In 1990 the Vermont legislature amended the tuition law to
permit elementary students from towns without a public school
to also attend private schools at the state's expense.[112] Meanwhile, a state legislator has drafted a bill to restrict state vouchers
to schools that accept the money as full payment for tuition.
These schools would also have to begin selecting students via
lottery. "Exclusive schools could still operate, but not at taxpayers' expense."[113]

One other significant development should be noted: the launch
of several privately funded voucher plans at the state and local
level. The first such program was started in Indianapolis in 1991
by the chairman of an insurance company, and beginning in the
1992–93 school year, dozens of businesses, private foundations,
and individual donors started providing low-income students in
Atlanta, Little Rock, and San Antonio with tuition money for
private and parochial schools.[114] These programs are less controversial because they do not use public funds to pay for private
schools, and they target low-income families, who are least likely
to have the means to attend private schools.

HOW FAR WILL THE POLITICAL POPULARITY
OF VOUCHERS TAKE US?

The political activity discussed in this chapter would lead most
readers to conclude that tuition vouchers for private schools—
equitable or not—are the wave of the future. It appears that

anti–public institution sentiment runs quite strong, and that many Americans are seeking private solutions to what used to be public problems. Thus, a growing number of advocates support private-school choice plans either because they apply a market metaphor to the educational system and are convinced that competition leads to improvement or because they believe strongly that individual families need maximum freedom in choosing schools.

Still, a major hurdle to wide-scale enactment of voucher programs remains, at least regarding those that include sectarian schools. We have yet to witness the passage of a private-school choice plan that does what many Americans consider to be the unthinkable: allows government funds to be spent on religious schools. The following chapter will explore the constitutional issues at stake in such a private-school choice program.

CHAPTER SIX

CONSTITUTIONAL ISSUES

VOUCHER PLANS AND

THE SEPARATION OF

CHURCH AND STATE

Many voters and policymakers who believe in the separation of church and state remain adamantly opposed to government-funded tuition voucher or tax credit programs. Because 81 percent of American private elementary and secondary schools are religious, policies allowing parents to spend government funds at any private school are perceived by opponents as a form of public support for religious instruction. These opponents argue that voucher plans in particular stand in clear violation of the First Amendment prohibition of the "establishment of religion," better known as the Establishment Clause, the underlying principle behind most church-state controversies in education.

Proponents of vouchers and tax credits claim that these programs do not violate the Establishment Clause because monies are given to parents and not directly to religious schools. They cite similar federal programs—including the G.I. Bill of Rights (1944) and the child-care provisions of Public Law 01-508 (1990) which provide tax credits and vouchers to parents who use church-run day-care centers—as evidence that private-school choice plans are constitutional. Furthermore, advocates argue that recent Supreme Court rulings indicate the Court's less stringent interpretation of the Establishment Clause.

This chapter lays out the political and legal arguments for and against public funding for parochial schools. Although this is primarily a federal issue—and has been historically—the debate has implications for state voucher or tax credit plans, especially since the constitutionality of many of these programs could be challenged in federal courts.

Legal rather than education goals are usually at stake in these debates, regardless of the educational goals espoused by those on either side. Still, those who oppose voucher plans on the basis of the First Amendment tend to support broader, democratic educational goals. They view voucher plans as divisive, channeling public money to educational institutions that often neglect to teach children to tolerate and respect people of different religious and ethnic backgrounds. These opponents argue that education is a public concern, not private, and that tax dollars should not pay for the education of students within private, ideologically specific institutions. On the other hand, proponents of tuition voucher plans who argue that it is not unconstitutional to spend public funds on religious schools tend to view the goal of education in terms of individual fulfillment in the more libertarian sense. They argue that parents have a legal "right" to control the education of their children, and to choose schools that develop specific religious beliefs and values in their children. Thus, they view education as serving private rather than public needs, and argue that while government should guarantee all children formal schooling, parents—not the government— should dictate what kind of schooling their children receive.

Perhaps the most interesting aspect of this debate is that, although voucher opponents make a strong argument concerning church-state issues and the democratic purpose of education, recent Supreme Court rulings in this area suggest that proponents could craft legislation giving parents public funds to spend at parochial schools and still pass constitutional muster. As Lawrence H. Tribe, an expert on constitutional law, has noted: "Any objection that anyone would have to a voucher program would have to be policy-based and could not rest on legal doctrine. One would have to be awfully clumsy to write voucher legislation that could not pass constitutional scrutiny."[1] The question, therefore, is whether those who oppose voucher plans for philosophical reasons can rely on constitutional arguments to prevent the enactment of these programs.

FEDERAL LAW AND RELIGIOUS SCHOOLS

I n 1875 President Ulysses S. Grant argued that "every child in the land may get a common school education unmixed with atheistic, pagan, or sectarian teaching." That same year, Congress considered a constitutional amendment banning the use of state funds for sectarian schools. The measure was passed by the House of Representatives, but failed to receive the necessary two-thirds vote required in the Senate.[2]

Still, the widening distinction between public and sectarian schools in the latter half of the 19th century and early 20th century and the anti–private school sentiment of President Grant and others reflected Protestant-versus-Catholic disputes over what was to be taught in publicly funded schools. Because the early common schools were, in most cases, founded and controlled by Protestants, the curriculum was far from secular and often included assignments from the King James Bible and the use of textbooks containing anti-Catholic statements.[3] This meant that non-Protestant families were forced to either accept the public schools' Protestant-based "moral education" or create private schools of their own.

In 1884 the Third Plenary Council of Catholic archbishops and bishops called for every Catholic parish that did not have a Catholic school to establish one: "No parish is complete till it has schools adequate to the needs of its children. . . ."[4] Furthermore, the council informed Catholic parents that they were "bound to send their children to the parish schools."[5] These efforts were not always well received. In the 1920s, Oregon voters passed an initiative that equated compulsory school attendance with compulsory *public* school attendance. Launched and supported by Protestant extremists—including the Ku Klux Klan—the initiative was an attempt to thwart efforts by Catholics and other non-Protestant religious groups to establish private schools. The Oregon law was challenged, and in 1925 the Supreme Court ruled in the case of *Pierce v. Society of Sisters* that parents had the right to send their children to private—religious or secular—schools.[6]

Even as the public school curriculum became increasingly secular by the middle of the 20th century, many Catholics preferred their own schools, referring to the public schools as "Protestant schools."[7] Meanwhile, growing numbers of upper-class Protestants were sending their children to elite private boarding schools, segregating them from both the masses in the burgeoning public system and the Catholic school students.[8]

The widening political and demographic rift between public and private schools presented a dilemma for federal policymakers whenever the issue of general aid to education was raised. Should aid be earmarked for all schools, or just public ones? In fact, prior to 1965 the issue of public aid to parochial schools remained the major stumbling block to the passage of laws allowing general federal assistance to elementary and secondary education. According to Bruce S. Cooper, education professor at Fordham University, whenever a federal assistance bill was introduced, supporters of private sectarian schools demanded their fair share of the money.[9]

The most vocal of such groups was the United States Catholic Conference (formerly known as the National Catholic Welfare Conference). Following World War II, the Catholic Conference opposed any federal school-aid bill that excluded Catholic schools.[10] The conference's position prompted the creation of a broad-based coalition of organizations against federal aid to parochial schools, most notably the National Education Association, the National Council of Churches, the American Jewish Congress, and various civil liberties groups including the American Civil Liberties Union.[11] The resulting stalemate doomed every proposal for general federal aid to education during the two decades following the war.

Even in 1949, when President Truman and members of both major parties endorsed the idea of general federal aid to elementary and secondary schools, a bill died in House subcommittee wrangling over whether the legislation should prohibit any form of assistance to private and parochial schools. A subsequent attempt, in 1950, by the House Committee on Education and Labor to overcome "the religious controversy" surrounding federal aid to education also failed when both sides agreed to kill the legislation.[12]

The political impasse continued into the early 1960s. With the education bill of 1961, President Kennedy asked for $2.3 billion for the construction of public school classrooms and increases in public school teachers' salaries as well as construction loans and student scholarships for public and private colleges. Aid to private elementary and secondary schools was barred, and the bill was defeated in Congress. In 1963 a similar education bill, also sponsored by President Kennedy and also barring aid to parochial schools, was defeated as well.[13]

Federal education legislation enacted prior to 1965 provided targeted funding, as opposed to general aid, and was available to both public and private schools. For instance, the Smith-Hughes Act of 1917 supplied federal funds to states to pay the salaries of teachers who taught agriculture, trades, industrial subjects, and home economics in public schools or "any kind of vocational" school. Although the act allowed federal funds to flow to private vocational schools, most of these schools at that time—especially those for blacks in the South—were supported by northern industrialists, not religious organizations.[14] The Smith-Hughes Act was also supposed to develop professional schools to train teachers in these subjects, but most of this teacher training money went to state normal schools and land-grant colleges and universities.[15]

The Servicemen's Readjustment Act of 1944, better known as the G.I. Bill of Rights, provided $14.5 billion in federal aid to World War II veterans who used the money to attend universities, colleges, high schools, trade schools, and training programs. The bill allocated funds for tuition, fees, books, and living expenses, money that could be spent at public or private (including religious) institutions. Veterans could apply to the schools of their choice, and the schools were free to control their admissions policies without federal intervention.[16] Despite the common perception that the G.I. Bill was used mainly for post-secondary education, only about 2.2 million of the almost eight million veterans served by the bill pursued higher education.[17]

Other legislation that made federal funds available to elementary and secondary schools included the National School Lunch Act of 1946, designed to reach children from low-income families whether they attended public, independent, or church-related institutions. The National Defense and Education Act of 1958 provided substantial federal support to secondary schools and institutions of higher learning to increase and upgrade defense-related course offerings, including science, math, engineering, and foreign languages. The aid was categorical, and many of the programs funded through the act were available to private, religious-affiliated schools.[18]

These programs, while not quite establishing general federal aid, somewhat blurred the distinction between public and private schools when it came to targeted federal programs.[19] Furthermore, in postwar years a number of local school systems authorized "shared-time," the practice of allowing parochial school students to attend public school classes on certain days each week.[20] And several indirect forms of public support to private schools were in place at the state level. In *Everson v. Board of Education* (1947), the Supreme Court ruled that a New Jersey township could reimburse parents for costs they incurred sending their children to parochial schools on public buses. In *Board of Education v. Allen* (1968), the Court upheld New York State's practice of lending state-approved secular textbooks to parochial schools.[21]

Despite these relatively small-scale, highly specific forms of federal and state funding, the major breakthrough in terms of the political impasse blocking federal aid to elementary and secondary education, both public and private, came in 1965 when President Johnson signed Public Law 89-10, better known as the Elementary and Secondary Education Act (ESEA). While this landmark legislation did not provide general aid for school construction or teachers' salaries, it did double the federal government's expenditures on education through five targeted or "categorical" programs—a form of funding that allowed a workable compromise on the issue of public aid to parochial schools.

Title 1, which received $1.06 billion of the bill's total $1.3 billion authorization, provided schools serving low-income students with grants for equipment, classroom construction, and additional staff. Nonpublic students could benefit from Title 1 through such services as educational radio and television, dual-employment programs between public and private schools, and "mobile" classrooms staffed by public school teachers. Title 2 provided a grant program for states to purchase library resources, instructional materials, and textbooks, which could be lent to local public or private school students.[22]

The political compromise that allowed ESEA to become law centered around what later came to be known as "the child-benefit theory," a policy distinction intended to sidestep the church-state issue by targeting funds directly to needy children and not to religious schools per se.[23] For instance, the largest program funded by the legislation, Title 1 (now Chapter 1), went to schools with high concentrations of low-income families. This tied educational aid—for public and parochial schools—to programs, and it was, therefore, politically difficult for groups like the NEA to fight the bill. In addition, Title 1 was to be administered through the public schools. This meant that federal funds were not flowing directly to private schools; instead, public school teachers were being sent to private schools to provide Title 1 services. The underlying philosophy was that the government was ultimately responsible for educating all children, even those attending private schools.

Federal and state funds for parochial schools, however indirect, peaked with ESEA. After 1965, Congress and the courts began rebuilding the wall between church-supported schools and public money. In fact, six years after the passage of ESEA, the Supreme Court set a tougher legal standard concerning public monies and the "establishment" of religion—a standard that would eventually have a strong impact on Title 1/Chapter 1 programs and private schools.

In *Lemon v. Kurtzman* (1971), the Court determined that basic guidelines and key rulings from previous decisions concerning the establishment of religion could best be summarized in a three-part test, which states that a statute or policy violates the Establishment Clause if *any one* of the following could be proved:

1. Its purpose is not secular;
2. Its principal/primary effect either advances or inhibits religion;
3. It fosters an excessive entanglement with religion.[24]

Since the *Lemon* decision, the most difficult legal questions concerning government assistance to private school students have typically arisen over the second part of the test, the issue of "primary effects." Most new public aid for religious schools has been disallowed since 1971 based on the argument that the "primary effect" of such aid is to advance religion. Relying on this second requirement of the *Lemon* test, major Supreme Court decisions during the past two decades have prohibited the allocation of federal or state assistance to private schools for salary supplements, field trips, instructional materials other than textbooks, auxiliary services, state-required tests, or remedial, guidance, and therapeutic services.[25]

In determining the "primary effects" of public aid to private schools, courts generally rely on two basic principles. First, the greater the number of people who benefit from a particular statute or policy, the more likely it is to be found constitutional. For instance, a public assistance program that benefits *all* private school students (not just those in parochial schools) is more likely to be upheld. If all students—both public and private—will benefit, there is an even greater likelihood that the program will be ruled constitutional.[26]

The second principle is based upon the identity of the "initial recipient" of the aid. In recent years, the Supreme Court has been much more receptive to policies that channel public aid to parochial school parents and students rather than directly to the schools themselves—a distinction made by those who drafted ESEA and the basis of one argument for the constitutionality of tuition voucher programs.[27]

Interestingly, though, the first case to effectively challenge the constitutionality of ESEA Chapter 1 programs that served private school students did not focus on the primary effects of the federal policy, but rather on the third part of the *Lemon* test: "excessive entanglement" between the state and religion. In *Aguilar v. Felton* (1985), the Supreme Court employed the entanglement argument to strike down the New York City Public Schools' use of federal funds to pay public school teachers to provide Chapter 1 services—remedial math and reading, ESL, and guidance—to low-income students in private schools.[28] (About 13 percent of the children eligible attended private schools. Of these, 84 percent were in Catholic schools and another 8 percent were enrolled in Hebrew day schools.[29]) Chapter 1 teachers were instructed to avoid religious involvement with any on-site religious activities and to keep contact with private school staff at a minimum. The monitoring of these teachers included frequent visits to participating parochial schools by program supervisors and coordinators.[30] The Court found that this monitoring violated the "excessive entanglement" test and created "an unconstitutional permanent and pervasive state presence" in these sectarian schools.[31]

The *Aguilar* decision led to substantial changes in the delivery of Chapter 1 services to low-income private school students. Public school districts that had been sending teachers into private schools before the ruling devised alternative methods of delivery, including public school–based programs, mobile vans, rented space near private schools, and electronic classroom technology.[32] In the last few years, a series of lower-court decisions concerning Chapter 1 funds and nonpublic schools have required states and school districts to deduct the extra cost of serving private school students "off the top" of their federal Chapter 1 allocations. In the most recent such case, *Pulido v. Cavazos* (1991), a three-judge panel of the U.S. Court of Appeals for the Eighth Circuit held unanimously that the U.S. Education Department could force states and districts to make these "off the top" deductions for private school students over objections from groups such as the National School Boards Association and Americans United for Separation of Church and State, who argued that this policy favors nonpublic school students and diverts federal tax dollars to religious schools.[33]

The *Lemon* decision has clearly had a profound impact on judicial rulings concerning public aid to private schools. But its influence is waning in the face of specific questions concerning the constitutionality of tuition vouchers and tax credits for parents who send their children to private schools.

AID TO PRIVATE SCHOOL PARENTS—TAX DEDUCTIONS, TAX CREDITS, AND TUITION VOUCHERS

Federal court cases pertaining to tax relief or other benefits to parents with children in private schools have resulted from challenges to state legislation. Two such cases have been appealed all the way to the U.S. Supreme Court and have led to landmark rulings concerning tax dollars and private schools—rulings that will have great bearing on whether tuition voucher plans that include religious schools will be held constitutional.

A 1973 case, *Committee for Public Education and Religious Liberty v. Nyquist*, provided the Supreme Court with its first opportunity to consider whether parents who were paying for private schools could be subsidized—through government reimbursements or tax breaks—for some or all of that expense. The

Committee for Public Education had challenged numerous provisions of a 1972 New York State law, including one establishing a program that provided "tuition reimbursements to parents of children attending elementary or secondary nonpublic schools" and a form of tax relief for those who failed to qualify for this reimbursement.[34] Under the "Elementary and Secondary Opportunity Program," parents with an annual taxable income of less than $5,000 (in 1972 dollars) would be reimbursed $50 for each elementary student and $100 for each high school student attending a private school. Parents with incomes greater than $5,000 but less than $25,000 would be allowed to subtract "a designated amount" from their adjusted gross income (on state income taxes) for each child attending a private school that charged at least $50 in tuition. Depending on family income, up to $1,000 could be deducted for each of as many as three dependents.[35]

While conceding that "not every law that confers an 'indirect,' 'remote,' or 'incidental' benefit upon religious institutions is, for that reason alone, constitutionally invalid," the Court found this New York program to be in violation of the Establishment Clause. Writing for the majority, Justice Lewis F. Powell, Jr., explained that both the tuition reimbursement and the tax credits failed to satisfy the second stipulation of the *Lemon* test, since the "primary effect" of the assistance would be to advance religion.[36] The Court determined that through both the tuition reimbursements and the tax benefits the state was relieving parents' financial burdens "sufficiently to assure that they continue to have the option to send their children to religion-oriented schools." The Court found, therefore, that "the effect of the aid is unmistakably to provide desired financial support for nonpublic, sectarian institutions."[37]

In this same case, the Court also considered whether the New York program constituted "excessive entanglement" and concluded that it did indeed provide parental assistance that "carries grave potential for entanglement in the broader sense of continuing political strife over aid to religion."[38]

The Supreme Court made fairly clear in *Nyquist* that a program of aid for *private school parents only* would be questionable, but it did not address programs that could potentially aid both public and private school parents. Consider, for instance, a voucher program like the one Californians will vote on in November 1993, which will give tuition "scholarships" to parents who choose either private schools or a new brand of independent public school. Given subsequent Supreme Court rulings in this area— including those discussed below—such a program now stands a better chance of surviving a constitutional challenge than the 1972 New York State law.

Ten years after *Nyquist*, the Supreme Court heard *Mueller v. Allen*. This case challenged a Minnesota statute that allowed parents state income tax deductions for educational expenses— tuition, textbooks, and transportation. Unlike the New York law, which was specifically targeted toward private school parents, this statute provided a tax deduction for all parents of K-12 students. Also, a cap was placed on the amount that parents could deduct: $500 per elementary school child and $700 per secondary school child (in 1982 dollars).[39]

Writing the majority opinion, Justice William H. Rehnquist explained that the most difficult question in the *Mueller* case arose over the second stipulation of the *Lemon* test: the need to determine whether the tax deduction has the "primary effect of advancing the sectarian aims of the nonpublic schools."[40] In this case, the Court was not persuaded by the plaintiff's contention that the Minnesota statute primarily benefited religious institutions, because all parents of K-12 students could take advantage of the tax deductions. In the *Mueller* decision, the Court held that Establishment Clause objections to the Minnesota law were invalid because the law channeled the assistance "through the *individual parents*" (emphasis added) and not directly to the schools. Public funds thus became available, the Court explained, "only as a result of numerous private choices of individual parents."[41]

On the issue of entanglement, the Court found that only a

minimal amount of monitoring (of textbooks) was required under the Minnesota program, and it did not qualify as excessive.[42] Therefore, the Court upheld the Minnesota program.

Since the *Mueller* decision, advocates of public/private school choice have argued that tuition voucher programs that give federal, state, or local money directly to parents instead of schools are indeed constitutional. According to John E. Coons of Berkeley, tuition voucher programs are legal because the choice of where to spend the money is made by the parents and not the state: "The state is not taking any position one way or the other where you ought to spend the voucher, which is different than the state giving money to a religious institution through a contract." Coons claims the situation is analogous to that of a state employee who is paid with state funds and uses money from his paycheck to make a donation to a religious institution. He argues that the same freedom ought to apply to parents who use state money to pay for their children's education.[43]

Those who oppose voucher programs say the *Mueller* decision does not indicate that voucher plans are constitutional, because tax deductions for school-related expenses are quite different from direct government aid or vouchers for private school tuition. "In the *Mueller* case, money was not given to parents to spend for education," said Lee Boothby, general counsel for Americans United for Separation of Church and State. "It was one of many deductions, like medical expenses . . . or a charitable deduction to a church."[44]

Despite this argument, a 1986 Supreme Court ruling in the case of *Witters v. Washington Department of Services for the Blind* provided tuition voucher advocates with more support. In this case, the Court considered whether Washington State's vocational rehabilitation assistance program was constitutional; it had been used to support a blind student who, at the time he applied for aid, was attending a private Christian college and seeking to become a pastor, missionary, or youth director.

As with similar cases, the Court based its Establishment Clause inquiry primarily on the second element of the *Lemon* test. In a unanimous decision, Justice Thurgood Marshall wrote that "the Establishment Clause is not violated every time money previously in the possession of a State is conveyed to a religious institution." He explained, however, that "the State may not grant aid to a religious school, whether cash or in kind, where the effect of the aid is 'that of a direct subsidy to the religious school' from the State." Interestingly, he then emphasized that aid may have such an effect if "it takes the form of aid to students or parents."[45] Marshall concluded that Washington's vocational rehabilitation assistance would not advance religion. Unlike other cases in which there was "no meaningful distinction between aid to the students and aid to the school," the case of this particular blind student appeared to be the only instance where state money would "end up flowing to religious education."[46]

The Court rejected the argument that such assistance was unconstitutional, finding that the Washington program was not "one of the ingenious plans for channeling state aid to sectarian schools." No financial incentive was created, they argued, "for students to undertake sectarian education. On the contrary, aid recipients have full opportunity to expend vocational rehabilitation aid on wholly secular education, and, as a practical matter, have rather greater prospects to do so."[47]

These recent decisions suggest that in the last ten years the Supreme Court has become increasingly lenient on the issue of public aid to parochial school students as long as the funds do not flow directly to the schools and benefit nonsectarian school students as well.

In fact, a growing number of jurists have come to criticize the *Lemon* test itself, labeling it "hostile to religion." Furthermore, according to Stuart Biegel, a professor of education law at UCLA, a majority of Supreme Court judges have stressed that while the *Lemon* criteria can be useful, they are not "willing to be confined to any single test" for Establishment Clause purposes.[48] In the *Mueller* decision, for instance, Justice Rehnquist declared that although "the general nature of . . . [the] inquiry in this area has been guided . . . by the three-part [*Lemon*] test,

. . . our cases have almost emphasized that it provides 'no more than a helpful signpost' in dealing with Establishment Clause challenges.''[49]

Biegel notes, for instance, that Justice Sandra Day O'Connor argues that Establishment Clause cases could be decided in a more precise and appropriate manner if the courts focused on whether a particular statute leads to governmental "endorsement" of religion. Declaring that a central tenet of Establishment Clause doctrine is the principle that the state must not make "adherence to a religion relevant in any way to a person's standing in the community," O'Connor asserts that "the government violates this prohibition if it endorses or disapproves of religion.''[50]

In 1989 the Supreme Court adopted this endorsement standard in the case of *County of Allegheny v. ACLU*, which focused on whether a crèche could be displayed in front of the county courthouse. The Court ruled that this Pennsylvania county had violated the Establishment Clause because the "principal or primary effect" of the crèche display constituted an endorsement equivalent to the promotion of religion.[51] In using this approach to test the constitutionality of a tuition voucher plan, the courts presumably ask whether a "reasonable observer" would perceive the policy as endorsing or promoting religion.

Meanwhile, according to Biegel, Justice Anthony M. Kennedy has begun to articulate a far less stringent Establishment Clause test, focusing on coercion. Kennedy's coercion framework would permit the government greater "latitude in recognizing and accommodating the central role religion plays in our society." Basically, a coercion test would include two limiting principles: First, the government may not coerce anyone to support or participate in religion and, second, the government may not give direct benefits to religion to such a degree that it in fact establishes religion.[52]

Many legal scholars believed that the 1992 Supreme Court case of *Lee v. Weisman* would mark a significant turning point in federal Establishment Clause jurisprudence.[53] In *Weisman*, the

Court considered for the first time the constitutionality of non-denominational invocation and benediction prayers at public high school graduation ceremonies. Both the defendant school board and the federal government urged the Court "to scrap . . . *Lemon*" in favor of a "coercion-of-religious-belief test" that would look more like what Justice Kennedy had been proposing.[54]

In one of the most unlikely decisions of recent years, however, the plaintiffs in *Weisman* won by a 5–4 vote. Instead of voting with the conservative wing of the Court to overturn the *Lemon* test, Justice Kennedy moved toward the philosophical center, writing the majority opinion, which found graduation prayers unconstitutional. In his opinion, he declared that there was no need in this case to "revisit" the controversy regarding the efficacy of overturning *Lemon v. Kurtzman*. "We can decide the [*Weisman*] case," Kennedy argued, "without reconsidering the general constitutional framework by which the public schools' efforts to accommodate religion are measured." He then went on to establish explicitly for the first time in a majority opinion that the First Amendment protected Americans from religious coercion by public entities. "It is beyond dispute," he wrote, "that, *at a minimum*, the Constitution guarantees that government may not coerce anyone to support or participate in religion or its exercise, or otherwise act in a way which 'establishes a [state] religion or religious faith, or tends to do so.' "[55]

The case was then decided under these "central principles" prohibiting coercion and establishment, and no further mention was made of the *Lemon* test, which the majority has now labeled "the general constitutional framework."[56]

It is unclear at this point what *Lee v. Weisman* might mean for prospective plaintiffs who declare that a school voucher program violates the Establishment Clause. Because this is the first school-related Establishment Clause case since 1971 that was not decided under the *Lemon* test but rather under a coercion analysis, it could signal a move toward a lower wall of separation between church and state. On the other hand, it could be argued that the *Weisman* coercion standard is simply an additional method for determining whether the second ("primary effect") part of *Lemon* has been violated.[57]

SHIFTING POLITICAL TIDES

As the legal doctrine on church-state issues moves toward a lower wall of separation, the political tides are turning as well. As was discussed earlier, the number of religious and private school organizations that support vouchers and tax credits continues to grow; the Catholic Conference and the National Catholic Education Association are now joined by many fundamentalist Christian educators in their support for public money for private schools.

Furthermore, in terms of constitutional issues, the federal child-care legislation of 1990 has provided the growing coalition of private-school choice supporters with more ammunition. The legislation provides grants to states to expand existing tax credit for parents who pay for child care and provides cash or vouchers for child care to low-income parents who could not work without such aid. Because nearly one-third of all child care is provided by religious organizations, Congress could not exclude sectarian centers from the aid package. It did, however, stipulate that church-based child-care centers were barred from using the federal money for sectarian purposes.[58]

Despite shifts in legal doctrine, an expanding political base for private school choice, and fallout from federal child-care legislation, opponents of federal aid to private school parents say they don't see the enactment of a federal voucher plan in the near future. These opponents—a mixture of "educational establishment" groups, including the two national teachers' unions, various civil rights groups, Americans United for Separation of Church and State, and the National Association for the Advancement of Colored People—argue that public aid for private child care is dramatically different from public aid to private elementary and secondary schools.

These voucher opponents cite two important differences: First, every state has a well-established public education system—something that has never existed at the preschool level—and, second, religious education or indoctrination is a much more significant issue for school-age children, who are forced to attend school under state compulsory attendance laws. Taxpayers, they claim, do not want to spend tax dollars on religious education.

Opponents of public aid to private schools also argue that, because the *Mueller* case concerned tax deductions, not tax credits or vouchers, and the *Witters* case was about higher education, not elementary or secondary schools, the First Amendment argument against private-school choice plans still holds. In addition, they state that lawsuits challenging such legislation could be based on a variety of legal theories linked to alleged denials of equal educational opportunities—thus the First Amendment is not the only source for objection. Plaintiffs in such suits could make legal arguments based on Title VI of the Civil Rights Act of 1964, Title IX of the Educational Amendments of 1972, the 14th Amendment, or state equal protection clauses.[59]

Lee Boothby, general counsel for Americans United for Separation of Church and State, cites several specific "discriminatory" practices of religious schools, including prohibitions against hiring anyone outside that particular faith and either refusing to admit a child who is not a member of the faith or at least requiring the child to participate in religious activities. "Many [parochial schools] give preference to children who are members of the school's parish."[60]

Another strong possibility is that these political and legal battles over private school choice will be played out at the state rather than the federal level. In much the same way that abortion has become a state-by-state legislative issue, and has then been brought back to the national agenda through the federal courts, the toughest private-school choice battles will most likely be fought in statehouses across the country, especially given that 14 states have introduced private-school choice legislation in the last three years.[61]

Furthermore, while it does appear as though political support for private-school choice plans grew rapidly following publication of Chubb and Moe's book and former President Bush's endorsement of such programs, the election of President Clinton, who ran as an opponent of voucher programs, may signal that for many supporters of voucher plans, it is not a primary national issue. It is certainly not at all clear whether a federal tax credit or tuition voucher plan could get through Congress. Individual states, however, especially those with a large percentage of students in private schools, are far more likely to pass legislation or amendments that include some form of tax deduction, credit, or vouchers to offset tuition at parochial schools. When and if they do, the First Amendment legal arguments against such programs—provided these plans include public school parents and give money directly to the parents and not to the schools themselves—could quite possibly carry far less weight than most politicians and taxpayers currently think. Those who argue against private-school choice programs, therefore, would do better to focus on legal arguments based on equal educational opportunity as well as on more philosophical questions about what voucher plans would mean to public schools in a democratic society. Voters and taxpayers should not assume that just because a voucher program can potentially pass constitutional muster, it is the *right* system of educational funding and governance.

A fter more than 30 years of experimentation with various forms of choice in public education and numerous political and legal arguments over whether the government should allow parents to spend public funds at private schools, it would seem that educators, policymakers, parents, and taxpayers would have a clearer sense of the role school choice can play in improving our educational system and how far we as a nation want to go in providing individual choice. But educational policy proposals do not evolve in isolation, and the future of school choice programs in this country will no doubt be strongly influenced by the direction of a more general reform movement known as school "restructuring," which focuses on changing the structure and organization of schools. In fact, the school choice debate has played a prominent role in recent discussions of educational restructuring.

Fred M. Newmann, a professor at the University of Wisconsin-Madison who specializes in educational reform issues, cites parental choice in education as one of the 11 most popular restructuring proposals now being advanced. Others include those favoring greater school autonomy from district and state regulations on curriculum, hiring, and budget; teachers and parents sharing decision-making authority with school administrators; year-round schooling; and national certification of teachers.[1]

But Newmann notes that while many of these proposals seem

reasonable, and while some are even supported by empirical research, policymakers and educators have yet to articulate the "why" and the "what" behind them:

> Why should restructuring be expected to improve education for students? The implied "theory" behind many proposals seems grounded largely on the assumption that new organizational structures will increase either the commitment or the competence of teachers and students. . . . [T]his assumption leads to a second question: What particular kinds of commitments and competence should the new structures produce, or what is the content of restructuring? Structure without substantive purpose leads nowhere in particular. . . .[2]

What Newmann and other observers of educational reform efforts are quick to point out is that in focusing on structural changes—e.g., those affecting the amount of freedom parents and students have in choosing schools or the way in which public education monies are allocated in a competitive system—reformers and politicians often make wrong assumptions about how parents, students, teachers, and administrators will respond to these changes. Among private-school choice advocates, for example, there is an implicit assumption that all parents and students will shop for schools with the highest-quality instructional programs and will indeed demand schools with high standards and more challenging curricula. Educators will respond to this demand and the newly deregulated educational structure, the assumption goes, by improving their instructional offerings. Thus, competition in education will lead to significant and long-lasting educational reform.

These are two rather broad assumptions, and anyone who has talked to parents or students about the factors on which they base their school choices knows that several nonacademic variables, including closeness to home and familiarity with teachers and other students, also play a major role in school choice. On the supply side, there is evidence that educators frequently compete for students on the basis of nonacademic offerings such as impressive facilities or outstanding athletic programs. Thus, the relationship between the proposed structural change and the responses it might provoke remains relatively unexplored and is generally assumed to be monolithic.

Discussions of the goals of various structural reforms need to include an understanding of the "commitments and competencies" of the educators, parents, and students whom these changes will affect. Furthermore, Newmann's effort to locate the political popularity of choice in education within the broader context of reform, or "restructuring," assists critics and proponents of choice policies in seeing choice as simply one piece of a much more complex puzzle—one reform that could either enhance or marginalize concurrent restructuring efforts.

Some educational historians describe the current clamor for parental choice in education, as well as the larger restructuring movement Newmann describes, as part of a backlash against 100 years of increasing centralization of educational governance, first within large school districts and later at the federal and state levels. From this perspective, the move to give parents greater say in where their children go to school, much like providing parents and teachers with more authority in school governance, may represent a predictable swing of the pendulum back toward the form of local control prevalent during the common school era in the late 19th century.

As David Tyack of Stanford University has argued, throughout much of the 19th century newly formed public education was a highly decentralized system of mostly isolated rural, one-room schoolhouses. He attributes this in part to a deep-rooted American distrust of centralized government:

> When states did try to control districts, citizens resisted state encroachment on local prerogatives. . . .Thus there was "school-based management" and community control to a degree unimaginable in today's schools. Local trustees and parents selected the

teachers, supervised their work, and sometimes boarded them in their homes.[3]

By the turn of the 20th century, however, urbanization and the rapid growth of large urban school districts began the movement toward greater centralization of educational governance, as superintendents and boards of education in these areas created tightly controlled schools with standardized instruction. According to Tyack, the first generation of "professional educational leaders" emerged from the new schools of education during this period and, sharing a common faith in an education science, "advocated innovations that would produce efficiency, equity (in their own definition), accountability, and expertise." These "reformers" set out to centralize control of schools by consolidating small school districts, abolishing one-room schools, and creating elite boards of education. They built hierarchies of curriculum experts and supervisors to tell teachers how and what to teach. At the same time, curricula became more differentiated "to match with supposed differences of ability and economic destiny of students."[4] Teachers, parents, and students were thus shut out of the decision-making process. Parents had virtually no choice in where their children would attend school and teachers had little authority to determine what students would learn when they got there.

This centralization of power and control prevailed until the 1960s and 1970s, when formerly disfranchised groups—African-Americans, women, the handicapped, non-English speakers—demanded a greater role in educational decision making and greater access to school resources and programs. And in one of the most notable paradoxes in American educational history, these efforts by reformers to decentralize educational governance led to an increased role for state and federal governments, as many school administrators resisted demands for equal access and greater involvement by formerly marginalized groups. As Tyack notes, efforts to create a more democratic, representative system resulted in larger, more complex, and more fragmented bureaucracies:

Finding local systems of schools resistant to their demands, out-
siders turned to higher levels of government—to state and federal
legislatures and courts—for redress. One result was increased
impact of federal and state governments on a system in which
decision making had remained largely a local prerogative well into
the 1950s. Legislatures and courts provided legal leverage for a
variety of reforms: racial desegregation, the attack on institutional
sexism, new bilingual programs, the introduction of ethnic curricula, new attention to the needs of the handicapped, and the
equalization of school finance.[5]

In addition to thousands of state and federal cases and their
resulting court orders, hundreds of laws were passed creating
categorical programs, each aimed at a different target population
of students—e.g., low-income, handicapped, bilingual—and
each requiring excessive monitoring. Thus, what Tyack calls
"midmanagers" were then needed at the district level to act as
accountants and watchdogs over these new state and federal
categorical programs.

Ironically, during this period of growth for alternative schools
within public education and greater parental and student choice
in terms of elective courses and nontraditional settings, much
decision making at the district level—including determinations
governing the flow of money and resources to schools—was being
dictated by the guidelines of state and federal programs. This
odd combination led to what Tyack and other historians have
termed "fragmented centralization"—"everybody and nobody
was in charge of public schooling. . . ."[6]

The emergence of the back-to-basics, excellence movement of
the 1980s allowed state governments and business coalitions to
add an additional layer of demands—for higher standards, stiffer
graduation requirements, and increased testing—thus creating
yet another reason to maintain centralized school governance,
particularly at the state level. As mentioned earlier, to a large
extent these reforms reduced the choices available to parents and
students within the public system.

Analysis of the push and pull between centralization and decentralization during these four periods may seem academic to some, but such considerations remain highly significant to understanding how we got to where we are today and why school choice policy, as part of a larger effort to restructure schools and decentralize decision-making power, needs to be thoughtfully constructed. For instance, when tuition voucher advocates who call for total deregulation of the educational system argue that the burgeoning bureaucracies of many public school districts stifle the creative genius of stellar teachers and administrators, they are correct for the most part. But we cannot tear down a highly regulated system without first considering why this system came to be—with particular focus on the resistance of local administrators to efforts by formerly marginalized groups to gain access to decision-making power within a system that had once shut them out.

Furthermore, to assume, as private-school choice advocates frequently do, that a competitive, deregulated, decentralized educational market will solve the problems of our troubled urban schools is naive at the very least. After all, lack of competition among schools did not *create* educational bureaucracies or the decline of urban education. Urban school districts, which have for the last 50 years competed heavily with suburban school districts and private schools for high-achieving students from wealthy backgrounds, have larger bureaucracies than most. They also provide far greater public school choice than either suburban or rural districts. But because they also receive far more of the federal and state categorical education money than districts and schools serving wealthier constituents, they are forced to deal with all of the attendant regulations. While a completely "deregulated" educational market in which each autonomous school competed for students would no doubt be less bureaucratized, it would also eliminate important guidelines that ensure all students the educational services they are entitled to by law.

Furthermore, certain inconsistencies are inherent in the current restructuring movement—i.e., the call for a set of national standards and tests side by side with demands for more school-site management and parental choice. If Washington, D.C., is dictating what students learn and when they learn it by imposing national standards and a set of national tests to make sure schools follow suit, what form of school choice does any parent or child have, and how much autonomy can teachers have to make decisions about what curriculum? Given that President Clinton and his Education Secretary both favor national standards, we may be headed for another era of fragmented centralization.

Thus, a caution: It is important to look back when planning to move ahead. Policymakers cannot allow us to slip back to a time when access and equity were left to the whims and good will of educators and their local patrons. While this larger move toward decentralization may have the potential to create more democratic forms of governance and empower formerly shut-out groups of parents and students, reforms must not move ahead in disregard of the battles fought thus far. Reform leaders will, hopefully, be guided by a vision of democratic public schools for the common good—schools aimed at helping every student succeed. Only then will the phrase "school choice" have real meaning.

CHAPTER ONE

1. According to the latest Gallup–Phi Delta Kappan Poll on attitudes toward education, only 17 percent of the public think there is anything terribly wrong with the schools in their own communities. See Karen De Witt, "Public in Poll Backs Change in Education," *The New York Times*, 28 August 1992, A7.

2. William Celis, 3rd, "Governors Find School Improvements Hard to Sell," *The New York Times*, 5 August 1992, A13.

3. As quoted in Henry J. Perkinson, *Two Hundred Years of American Educational Thought* (New York: David M. McKay Company, 1976), 63.

4. Ibid., 64.

5. See Joel Spring, *The American Public School, 1642–1990*, 2nd ed. (White Plains, N.Y.: Longman, 1990), 90–91.

6. Ibid., 89.

7. As cited in Perkinson, *Two Hundred Years of American Educational Thought*, 86.

8. See Carl Kaestle, *Pillars of the Republic: Common Schools and American Society, 1780–1860* (New York: Hill and Wang, 1983).

9. See David Hogan, "Markets and the Demand for Education," *Educational Policy* 6 (2) (June 1992): 180–205.

10. See Ellen Condliffe Lagemann, "The Plural Worlds of Educational Research," *History of Education Quarterly* 29 (2) (Summer 1989): 185–214.

11. Ibid., 199.

12. Perkinson, *Two Hundred Years of American Educational Thought*, 202.

NOTES

13. Kenneth A. Strike, "The Moral Role of Schooling in a Liberal Democratic Society," *Review of Research in Education* 17 (1990): 413–83.
14. Quoted in Lagemann, "The Plural Worlds of Educational Research," 199.
15. John Dewey, *Experience and Education* (New York: The Macmillan Company, 1938), 31.
16. Amy Gutmann, *Democratic Education* (Princeton, N.J.: Princeton University Press, 1987), xi.
17. Ibid., 42.
18. Ibid., 43.
19. Ibid.
20. Ibid., 45.
21. Ibid., 162.
22. Such public dialogues—manifested in actions as simple as voting for elected education officials or choosing candidates at least partly on the basis of their education policy proposals—are restricted mainly to issues concerning public education, not private education, which is generally operated based upon succinctly nonpublic principles.
23. Henry A. Giroux, "Educational Leadership and the Crisis of Democratic Government," *Educational Researcher* 21 (4) (May 1992): 8.
24. Edward B. Fiske, *Smart Schools, Smart Kids: Why Do Some Schools Work?* (New York: Simon & Schuster, 1991), 59–61.
25. Ibid., 60.
26. Ann Bradley, "Poll Highlights Positive Response to Chicago Reforms," *Education Week* (10 February 1993), 5.
27. See Michelle Fine, "[AP]parent Involvement: Reflections on Parents, Power, and Urban Public Schools," *Teachers College Record* 94 (4) (Summer 1993): 682–709, and Sandy Banks and Stephanie Chavez, "L.A. Schools O.K. Historic Reforms," *Los Angeles Times*, 16 March 1993, A1, A3.
28. See Strike, "Moral Role of Schooling," 431.
29. Ibid., 440.
30. Quoted in Perkinson, *Two Hundred Years of American Educational Thought*, 127.
31. See Strike, "Moral Role of Schooling," 437, for a discussion of liberalism and transgenerational dominance.
32. Quoted in Perkinson, *Two Hundred Years of American Educational Thought*, 128.
33. Lawrence A. Cremin, *The Transformation of the School: Pro-*

gressivism in American Education, 1876–1957 (New York: Vintage Books, 1964), 104. For a discussion of G. Stanley Hall's and Cremin's views on progressivism see Thomas Toch, *In the Name of Excellence: The Struggle to Reform the Nation's Schools, Why It's Failing and What Should Be Done* (New York: Oxford University Press, 1991), 44–54.

34. See Diane Ravitch, *The Troubled Crusade: American Education, 1945–1980* (New York: Basic Books, 1983), 44, 47.
35. See Cremin, *Transformation of the School*, 22, and Ravitch, *Troubled Crusade*, 45–47.
36. See Ravitch, *Troubled Crusade*, 50–55, and Toch, *In the Name of Excellence*, 49–51.
37. Dewey, *Experience and Education*, 6.
38. Ibid., 34.
39. Ravitch, *Troubled Crusade*, 47.
40. David Tyack, " 'Restructuring' in Historical Perspective: Tinkering Toward Utopia," *Teachers College Record* 92 (2) (Winter 1990): 177–79.
41. Toch, *In the Name of Excellence*, 7.
42. See Ivan Illich, *Deschooling Society* (New York: Harper and Row, 1970); Gutmann, *Democratic Education*, 278; and Perkinson, *Two Hundred Years of American Educational Thought*, 309.
43. See Toch, *In the Name of Excellence*, 7.
44. Gutmann, *Democratic Education*, 28–33.
45. Ibid., 29.
46. Cited in Spring, *American School*, 79.
47. Toch, *In the Name of Excellence*, 49.
48. Ravitch, *Troubled Crusade*, 229.
49. See Spring, *American School*, 326.
50. Ravitch, *Troubled Crusade*, 229.
51. See Spring, *American School*, 336.
52. Ibid., 345.
53. National Commission on Excellence in Education, *A Nation at Risk* (Washington, D.C., 1983), 6–7.
54. Toch, *In the Name of Excellence*, 20.
55. Ibid., 15, 20, 21.
56. Cited in Jonathan Weisman, "Educators Watch with a Wary Eye as Business Gains Policy Muscle," *Education Week* (31 July 1991), 25.
57. Ibid.
58. George R. Kaplan and Michael D. Usdan, "The Changing

Look of Education's Policy Networks," *Phi Delta Kappan* 73 (9) (May 1992): 668.

59. Ibid., 671.

60. See Henry A. Giroux and Peter McLaren, "America 2000 and the Politics of Erasure: Democracy and Cultural Difference Under Siege," *International Journal of Educational Reform* (forthcoming, 1993), and Henry A. Giroux and Peter McLaren, "Teacher Education and the Politics of Engagement: The Case for Democratic Schooling," *Harvard Education Review* 56 (3) (August 1986): 213–38.

61. Jesse Kornbluth, "Chris and Benno's Excellent Adventure," *Vanity Fair*, August 1992, 146.

62. *The New York Times*, "Judge Denies Bid to Close In-School TV Program," 10 September 1992, A19.

63. Kornbluth, "Chris and Benno's Excellent Adventure," 142–76.

64. *The New York Times*, "Judge Denies Bid . . . ," A19.

65. Kornbluth, "Chris and Benno's Excellent Adventure," 172, and Walsh, Mark, "Whittle to Ask to Exceed Daily Limit of 2 minutes for Ads on Channel One," *Education Week* (2 June 1993), 4.

66. Deborah Sontag, "Yale President Quitting to Lead National Private-School System," *The New York Times*, 26 May 1992, A1, A12.

67. Kornbluth, "Chris and Benno's Excellent Adventure," 145.

68. See Susan Chira, "Whittle's School Unit Gains Prestige and Pressure," *The New York Times*, 27 May 1992, B6, and William Celis, 3rd, "Private Group Hired to Run Nine Public Schools in Baltimore," *The New York Times*, 11 June 1992, A14.

CHAPTER TWO

1. National Center for Education Statistics, *Digest of Education Statistics, 1991* (Washington, D.C.: U.S. Department of Education, Office of Educational Research and Improvement, November 1991), 93.

2. Jonathan Kozol, *Free Schools* (Boston: Houghton Mifflin, 1972), 16.

3. Bonnie Barrett Stretch, "The Rise of the 'Free School,' " *Saturday Review*, 20 June 1970, 76–79, 90–94.

4. See Carl Weinberg, "The Meaning of Alternatives," in *The*

Conventional and the Alternative in Education, ed. John Good-lad (Berkeley, Calif.: McCutchan Publishing, 1973), 49–76, or Kozol, *Free Schools*.

5. Weinberg, "The Meaning of Alternatives," 73.
6. Jerry Mintz, *National Directory of Alternative Schools* (Glen-moore, Pa.: National Coalition of Alternative Community Schools, 1987).
7. A. S. Neill, *Summerhill: A Radical Approach to Child Rearing* (New York: Hart Publishing, 1960), 4.
8. See Thomas Toch, *In the Name of Excellence* (New York: Oxford University Press, 1991), 47.
9. Joel Spring, *Education and the Rise of the Corporate State* (Boston: Beacon Press, 1972).
10. Ibid., 145.
11. Joel Spring, *The American School, 1642–1990*, 2nd ed. (White Plains, N.Y.: Longman, 1990), 367.
12. John Dewey, *The School and Society*, 11th ed. (Chicago: University of Chicago Press, 1971), 21.
13. David Tyack, " 'Restructuring' in Historical Perspective: Tinkering Toward Utopia," *Teachers College Record* 92 (2) (Winter 1990): 177–79.
14. Spring, *Education and the Rise of the Corporate State*, 148.
15. Spring, *The American School*, 367–68.
16. Lawrence A. Cremin, "The Free School Movement: A Perspective," in *Alternative Schools: Ideologies, Realities, Guidelines*, ed. T. E. Deal and R. R. Nolan (Chicago: Nelson-Hall, 1978), 203–11.
17. Stretch, "The Rise of the 'Free School,' " 76.
18. Ibid., 76.
19. See Terrence E. Deal and Robert R. Nolan, "An Overview of Alternative Schools," in *Alternative Schools: Ideologies, Realities, Guidelines*, 1–18, and Weinberg, "The Meaning of Alternatives."
20. Mary Anne Raywid, "Alternative Education: The Definition Problem," *Changing Schools* 22 (3) (September 1990): 4–5, 10.
21. Stretch, "The Rise of the 'Free School,' " 76.
22. Ibid., 78.
23. Christopher Jencks, "Giving Parents Money to Pay for Schooling: Education Vouchers," *The New Republic*, 4 July 1970, 19–21.
24. Christopher Jencks, "Giving Parents Money for Schools: Ed-

ucation Vouchers," *Phi Delta Kappan* 111 (1) (September 1970): 49–52.

25. See R. G. Bridge and J. Blackman, *A Study of Alternatives in American Education*, vol. 4: *Family Choice in Schooling*, Report Number R-2170-NIE (Santa Monica, Calif.: The Rand Corporation, 1978).

26. See Tyack, " 'Restructuring' in Historical Perspective," 179–81.

27. Ibid., 180.

28. David Tyack and Elizabeth Hansot, *Managers of Virtue: Public School Leadership in America, 1820–1980* (New York: Basic Books, 1982).

29. Vernon H. Smith, *Alternative Schools: The Development of Options in Public Education* (Lincoln, Neb.: Professional Educators' Publications, Inc., 1974).

30. National School Public Relations Association, *Alternative Schools: Why, What, Where, and How Much.* Education U.S.A. Special Report (Arlington, Va., 1980).

31. Smith, *Alternative Schools.*

32. See Mario Fantini, *Public Schools of Choice* (New York: Simon & Schuster, 1973), and Mary Anne Raywid, "Choice Orientations, Discussions, and Prospects," *Educational Policy* 6 (2) (June 1992): 107.

33. Council of Big City Boards of Education, "Survey of Public Education in the Nation's Big City School Districts" (Washington, D.C.: National School Boards Association, 1975).

34. Spring, *The American School*, 368.

35. See Mario Fantini, "Alternatives in the Public Schools," in *Alternative Schools: Ideologies, Realities, Guidelines*, 49–58.

36. Smith, *Alternative Schools*, 14.

37. Thomas E. Wolf, Michael Walker, and Robert A. Mackin, *Summary of the NASP Survey 1974* (Amherst: University of Massachusetts, 1975).

38. NSPRA, *Alternative Schools*, 10.

39. Ibid., 11.

40. See Mary Frances Crabtree, "Chicago's Metro High: Freedom, Choice, Responsibility," in *Alternative Schools: Ideologies, Realities, Guidelines*, 91–96.

41. See Smith, *Alternative Schools*, 16.

42. Wolf et al., *Summary of the NASP Survey.*

43. See Smith, *Alternative Schools*, and Mary Anne Raywid,

"Schools of Choice: Their Current Nature and Prospects," *Phi Delta Kappan* 64 (10) (June 1983): 684–88.

44. Smith, *Alternative Schools*.
45. Raywid, "Schools of Choice."
46. Joan Chesler, "Innovative Governance Structures in Secondary Schools," reprinted in *Alternative Schools: Ideologies, Realities, Guidelines*, 287.
47. Cited in Deal and Nolan, "An Overview of Alternative Schools," 4.
48. See Raywid, "Alternative Education."
49. Toch, *In the Name of Excellence*, 56.
50. Ibid.
51. Cited in Toch, *In the Name of Excellence*, 57.
52. Ibid., 206.
53. See Timothy W. Young, *Public Alternative Education: Options and Choices for Today's Schools* (New York: Teachers College Press, 1990).
54. Ibid., 16.
55. See Raywid, "Alternative Education."
56. Young, *Public Alternative Education*, 20.
57. Ibid., 19–20.
58. Robert D. Barr, "The Growth of Alternative Public Schools: The 1975 ICOPE Report," *Changing Schools* (12) (1975): 1–15.
59. Mary Anne Raywid, "Family Choice Arrangements in Public Schools: A Review of the Literature," *Review of Educational Research* 55 (4) (Winter 1985), 460.
60. Educational Research Service, Inc., *Evaluation of Alternative Schools* (Arlington, Va., 1977), 44.
61. Ibid.
62. Cited in Young, *Public Alternative Education*, 40.
63. Ibid., 42.
64. Vernon Smith, Daniel J. Burke, and Robert D. Barr, *Optional Alternative Public Schools* (Bloomington, Ind.: Phi Delta Kappa Educational Foundation, 1974), 13.
65. ERS, *Evaluation of Alternative Schools*.
66. Raywid, "Schools of Choice."
67. Ibid., 685.
68. Ibid., 686.
69. Seymour Fliegel, "Creative Non-Compliance in East Harlem Schools." Paper presented at the Conference on Choice and

Control in American Education, University of Wisconsin-Madison, 1989.

70. For more information on the elementary schools and Central Park East Secondary School see Deborah Meier, "Central Park East: An Alternative Story," *Phi Delta Kappan* (June 1987): 753–57.

71. Ibid., 754.

72. Seymour Fliegel, "Choosing Your Public School," *Education: The Consumer's View* (Washington, D.C.: Educational Excellence Network, 1992), 6.

73. Fliegel, "Choosing Your Public School."

74. Carnegie Foundation for the Advancement of Teaching, *School Choice: A Special Report* (Ewing, N.J., 1992).

75. See National Commission on Excellence in Education, *A Nation at Risk: The Imperative for Educational Reform* (Washington, D.C., 1983).

76. See Edward B. Fiske, *Smart Schools, Smart Kids: Why Do Some Schools Work?* (New York: Simon & Schuster, 1991).

77. William Celis, 3rd, "Denver Plans to Shut Its Alternative School," *The New York Times*, 20 May 1992, B8.

78. Ibid.

79. Robert Ferris, "From Gadfly to Mainstream: The New Orleans Free School 20 Years Later," *National Coalition News* 16 (1) (Spring 1991): 14.

CHAPTER THREE

1. Gary Orfield, *Must We Bus? Segregated Schools and National Policy* (Washington, D.C.: The Brookings Institution, 1978).

2. Mark G. Yudof, David L. Kirp, and Betsy Levin, *Educational Policy and the Law*, 3rd ed. (St. Paul: West Publishing Company, 1992), 483.

3. Christine Rossell, *The Carrot or the Stick for School Desegregation Policy: Magnet Schools or Forced Busing* (Philadelphia: Temple University Press, 1990), 4.

4. Cited in Ibid., 5.

5. Yudof et al., *Educational Policy and the Law*, 483.

6. This quote was cited in Rossell, *Carrot or the Stick*, 5, and in Gary Orfield, *The Reconstruction of Southern Education: The Schools and the 1964 Civil Rights Act* (New York: Wiley-Interscience, 1969), 128.

7. Orfield, *Reconstruction of Southern Education*, 136.

8. Ibid., 135–37.
9. Ibid., 137–39.
10. See Rossell, *Carrot or the Stick*, 6.
11. Yudof et al., *Educational Policy and the Law*, 484.
12. Ibid., 485.
13. Ibid.
14. Ibid., 491.
15. See Willis Hawley, "Research, Public Opinion and Public Action: Thoughts on the Future of School Desegregation." Paper presented at the annual meeting of the American Educational Research Association, San Francisco, 1992.
16. Yudof et al., *Educational Policy and the Law*, 492–93.
17. Cited in Yudof et al., *Educational Policy and the Law*, 496.
18. Orfield, *Must We Bus?*, 15.
19. Yudof et al., *Educational Policy and the Law*, 499.
20. Ibid., 503.
21. Rossell, *Carrot or the Stick*, 4.
22. For more detail on the St. Louis Voluntary Transfer Plan see Amy Stuart Wells, Robert L. Crain, and Susan Uchitelle, *Stepping Over the Color Line: African-American Students in White Suburban Schools* (New Haven, Conn.: Yale University Press, forthcoming).
23. Gary Orfield and Franklin Monfort, *Status of School Desegregation: Next Generation*. Report to the National School Boards Association (Alexandria, Va.: National School Boards Association, 1992), 23.
24. Timothy W. Young, *Public Alternative Education: Options and Choices for Today's Schools* (New York: Teachers College Press, 1990), 16.
25. Joel Spring, *The American Public School, 1642–1990*, 2nd ed. (White Plains, N.Y.: Longman, 1990), 353.
26. Robert Dentler, "Conclusions from a National Study," in *Magnet Schools: Recent Developments and Perspectives*, ed. Nolan Estes, Daniel U. Levine, and Donald R. Waldrip (Austin, Tex.: Morgan Printing & Publishing, 1990), 62.
27. Ibid., 64.
28. See Rolf K. Blank, "Educational Effects of Magnet High Schools," in *Choice and Control in American Education*, vol. 2: *The Practice of Choice, Decentralization, and School Restructuring*, ed. William H. Clune and John F. Witte (New York: Falmer Press, 1990), 77–109.
29. Carol Ascher, "Using Magnet Schools for Desegregation:

Some Suggestions from the Research," in *Magnet Schools: Recent Developments and Perspectives*, 5.

30. Ibid.

31. Rolf K. Blank and Douglas A. Archbald, "Magnet Schools and Issues of Education Quality." Unpublished paper, July 1992.

32. General Accounting Office, *Magnet Schools: Information of the Grant Award Process*. Briefing Report to the Chairman, Committee on Labor and Human Resources, U.S. Senate (Washington, D.C., October 1987).

33. See Young, *Public Alternative Education*, 17.

34. Rossell, *Carrot or the Stick*, 122.

35. Ibid., 123.

36. Interview with Magnet School Coordinator, San Diego City Schools, May 1992.

37. For more information about San Diego magnet schools see E. Jean Brown, George Frey, Jan Garbosky, Nancy Shelburne, and Elizabeth A. Tomblin, "The Success of Magnet Schools: The San Diego Experience," in *Magnet Schools: Recent Developments and Perspectives*, 87–128, and San Diego City Schools, "Making Your Educational Dreams Come True," in *Magnet Programs Secondary Levels 1992–93* (San Diego, 1992).

38. Rossell, *Carrot or the Stick*, 113.

39. Los Angeles Unified School District, "Choices, 1992–93" (Los Angeles, 1992), 8.

40. Amy Stuart Wells, "Quest for Improving Schools Finds Role for Free Market," *The New York Times*, 14 March 1990, A1, B8.

41. Rossell, *Carrot or the Stick*, 137–45.

42. Cited in Amy Stuart Wells, "Once a Desegregation Tool, Magnet Schools Become Schools of Choice," *The New York Times*, 9 January 1991, B6.

43. Cited in Donald R. Moore and Suzanne Davenport, "School Choice: The New Improved Sorting Machine," in *Choice in Education: Potential and Problems*, ed. William Lowe Boyd and Herbert J. Walberg (Berkeley, Calif.: McCutchan Publishing, 1990), 187–223.

44. See Rolf K. Blank, Robert A. Dentler, D. C. Baltzell, and K. Chabotar, *Survey of Magnet Schools: Analyzing a Model for Quality Integrated Education*. Final Report of a National

Study for the U.S. Department of Education (Washington, D.C.: James H. Lowry and Associates, 1983).

45. Wells, "Once a Desegregation Tool."
46. Blank, "Educational Effects of Magnet High Schools," 91.
47. Robert L. Crain, Amy L. Heebner, and Yiu-Pong Si, *The Effectiveness of New York City's Career Magnet Schools: An Evaluation of Ninth Grade Performance Using an Experimental Design* (Berkeley, Calif.: National Center for Research in Vocational Education, 1992).
48. Moore and Davenport, "School Choice: The New Improved Sorting Machine."
49. Ibid., 197.
50. Ibid.
51. Ibid., 199.
52. Blank and Archbald, "Magnet Schools and Issues of Education Quality," 4.
53. Wells, "Once a Desegregation Tool."
54. Blank, "Educational Effects of Magnet High Schools."
55. See Rossell, *Carrot or the Stick*, 111–20.
56. Young, *Public Alternative Education*, 34.
57. Orfield, *Must We Bus?*, 405.
58. Jeffrey Henig, "Choice in Public Schools: An Analysis of Requests Among Magnet Schools," *Social Science Quarterly* 71 (1) (March 1990): 69–82.
59. The Carnegie Foundation for the Advancement of Teaching, *School Choice: A Special Report* (Ewing, N.J., 1992), 35.
60. Blank, "Educational Effects of Magnet High Schools."
61. Carnegie Foundation, *School Choice*, 36.
62. See Charles V. Willie, "Controlled Choice: An Alternative Desegregation Plan for Minorities Who Feel Betrayed," *Education and Urban Society* 23 (2) (February 1991): 206.
63. See Michael J. Alves and Charles V. Willie, "Choice, Decentralization and Desegregation: The Boston 'Controlled Choice' Plan," in *Choice and Control in American Education*, vol. 2: *The Practice of Choice, Decentralization, and School Restructuring*, 17–75.
64. Carnegie Foundation, *School Choice*, 36.
65. Ibid., 25.
66. Ibid., 204.
67. Quoted in Ellen Condliffe Lagemann, "The Plural Worlds of Educational Research," *History of Education Quarterly* 29 (2) (Summer 1989): 199.

NOTES

CHAPTER FOUR

1. For a detailed description of Governor Perpich's education reforms see Tim Mazzoni and Barry Sullivan, "Legislating Educational Choice in Minnesota: Politics and Prospects," in *Choice in Education: Potential and Problems*, ed. William L. Boyd and Herbert J. Walberg (Berkeley, Calif.: McCutchan Publishing, 1990), 149–76.

2. Minnesota House of Representatives Research Department, *The Postsecondary Enrollment Options Program: A Research Report* (St. Paul, February 1993), 50–59.

3. Recent figures on the costs and participation rates in the Minnesota statewide choice plans came from telephone interviews with either Steve Ethridge or Peggy Hunter, both with the Minnesota Department of Education, June 1992, and Minnesota House of Representatives, *The Postsecondary Enrollment Options Program*, 48.

4. Joe Nathan and Wayne Jennings, *Access to Opportunity: Experiences of Minnesota Students in Four Statewide School Choice Programs, 1989–90* (Minneapolis: Center for School Change, Hubert H. Humphrey Institute of Public Affairs, 1990).

5. Carnegie Foundation for the Advancement of Teaching, *School Choice: A Special Report* (Ewing, N.J., 1992), 52.

6. Judith Pearson, *The Myths of Educational Choice* (New York: Praeger, 1993), 26–27.

7. Ibid.

8. Jessie Montano, "Choice Comes to Minnesota," in *Public Schools by Choice: Expanding Opportunities for Parents, Students, and Teachers*, ed. Joe Nathan (St. Paul: Institute for Learning and Teaching, 1989), 171.

9. Ibid., 172.

10. Ibid., 174.

11. Ibid., 175–76.

12. Ibid., 175–78.

13. Ibid., 175.

14. Interview with Steve Ethridge, Minnesota Department of Education, June 1993.

15. Minnesota House of Representatives, *The Postsecondary Enrollment Options Program*, 13.

16. Nathan and Jennings, *Access to Opportunity*.

17. Ibid., 14, and Policy Studies Associates, Inc., *Minnesota's Open Enrollment Option* (Washington, D.C., 1992).
18. Nathan and Jennings, *Access to Opportunity*, 13.
19. Ibid., 12.
20. Minnesota House of Representatives, *The Postsecondary Enrollment Options Program*, 29.
21. Ibid., 31.
22. Ibid., 35.
23. Nathan and Jennings, *Access to Opportunity*, 21.
24. Pearson, *Myths of Educational Choice*, 25.
25. Nathan and Jennings, *Access to Opportunity*, 23.
26. Personal correspondence, July 1992.
27. Edward B. Fiske, *Smart Sch‿ols, Smart Kids: Why Do Some Schools Work?* (New York: Simon & Schuster, 1991), 193.
28. Joe Nathan, "Progress, Problems, and Prospects with State Choice Plans," in *Public Schools by Choice*, 203–24.
29. American Legislative Exchange Council, *Legislative Update* (Washington, D.C., February 24, 1992).
30. Nathan and Jennings, *Access to Opportunity*, 7.
31. Policy Studies Associates, Inc., *Minnesota's Educational Options for At-Risk Youth: Urban Alternative Schools and Area Learning Centers* (Washington, D.C., 1992), iv.
32. Nathan and Jennings, *Access to Opportunity*, 13.
33. Ibid., and Policy Studies Associates, *Minnesota's Educational Options for At-Risk Youth*, iii.
34. Nathan and Jennings, *Access to Opportunity*, 14.
35. Policy Studies Associates, *Minnesota's Educational Options for At-Risk Youth*, 8.
36. Ibid., 17.
37. Nathan and Jennings, *Access to Opportunity*, 24.
38. Ibid., 2.
39. Nathan, "Progress, Problems, and Prospects with State Choice Plans," 205–7.
40. Carnegie Foundation, *School Choice: A Special Report*, 11–12.
41. For details regarding these restrictions see Mazzoni and Sullivan, "Legislating Educational Choice."
42. See Mazzoni and Sullivan, "Legislating Educational Choice."
43. Policy Studies Associates, *Minnesota's Open Enrollment Option*.
44. Carnegie Foundation, *School Choice: A Special Report*, 13.
45. See Fiske, *Smart Schools*, 191.
46. Ibid., and Pearson, *Myths of Educational Choice*, 38.

47. Carnegie Foundation, *School Choice: A Special Report*, 25–26.
48. Pearson, *Myths of Educational Choice*, 33.
49. Policy Studies Associates, *Minnesota's Open Enrollment Option*, 12–13.
50. Personal correspondence, July 1992.
51. Nathan and Jennings, *Access to Opportunity*, 1.
52. Policy Studies Associates, *Minnesota's Open Enrollment Option*, 38.
53. The description of Cyrus comes from Fiske, *Smart Schools*, 192.
54. Policy Studies Associates, *Minnesota's Open Enrollment Option*, 50–51.
55. Carnegie Foundation, *School Choice: A Special Report*, 13.
56. Isabel Wilkerson, "Des Moines Acts to Halt White Flight After State Allows Choice of Schools," *The New York Times*, 16 December 1992, A15.
57. Karen Diegmueller, "Massachusetts Education Panel Votes to Repeal Choice Law," *Education Week*, 13 May 1992, 17.
58. Carnegie Foundation, *School Choice: A Special Report*, 26–27.
59. Peter Schmidt, "Massachusetts Districts Turn Thumbs Down on State's Hastily Passed Choice Program," *Education Week*, 11 September 1991, 1, 17.
60. Ibid.
61. Carnegie Foundation, *School Choice: A Special Report*, 59.
62. Ted Kolderie, "The Charter Schools Idea," *Public Services Redesign Project* (St. Paul: Center for Policy Studies, June 18, 1992).
63. Ibid., 4.
64. Ibid., 5, 6.
65. Ibid., 10–11.
66. "Minnesota Board Issues First Rejection of 'Charter' School," *Education Week*, 29 April 1992, 2.
67. A group of UCLA researchers, Amy Stuart Wells, Amanda Datnow, and Diane Hirshberg, are currently studying the politics of the charter school application process in the Los Angeles area.

CHAPTER FIVE

1. National Catholic Education Association, "The People's Poll on Schools and School Choice: A New Gallup Survey," Ex-

ecutive Summary (Washington, D.C., September 17, 1992).

2. See Millicent Lawton, "Gallup Poll Finds Wide Support for Tuition Vouchers," *Education Week*, 23 September 1992, 1, 16.

3. David Tyack and Elizabeth Hansot, *Managers of Virtue: Public School Leadership in America, 1820–1980* (New York: Basic Books, 1982), 29.

4. E. Eidenberg and R. D. Morey, *An Act of Congress: The Legislative Process and the Making of Education Policy* (New York: W. W. Norton & Company, 1969), 10.

5. David B. Tyack, "The Public Schools: A Monopoly or a Contested Public Domain?" in *Choice and Control in American Education*, vol. 1. *The Theory of Choice and Control in American Education*, ed. William H. Clune and John F. Witte (New York: Falmer Press, 1990), 89.

6. Henry M. Levin, "The Theory of Choice Applied to Education," in *Choice and Control in American Education*, 251.

7. Ibid.

8. See Amy Gutmann, *Democratic Education* (Princeton, N.J.: Princeton University Press, 1987), 116.

9. Peter W. Cookson, Jr., "The Rise of the Private School: The Implications for the Redesign of American Education." Paper presented at "Choice: What Role in American Education?": a symposium sponsored by the Economic Policy Institute, Washington, D.C. (1 October 1992). (Papers presented at this symposium to be published in *Choice: What Role in American Education?* [Washington, D.C.: Economic Policy Institute, forthcoming].)

10. Amy Gutmann, *Democratic Education*, 118.

11. Anthony S. Bryk and Valerie Lee, "Lessons from Catholic High Schools on Renewing Our Educational Institutions." Paper presented at "Choice: What Role in American Education?"

12. Michelle Fine, "Democratizing Choice: Reinventing Public Education." Paper presented at "Choice: What Role in American Education?," 2.

13. Fine, "Democratizing Choice," 2–3.

14. See, for instance, John Witte, "The Milwaukee Private-School Parental Choice Program." Paper presented at "Choice: What Role in American Education?"

15. See, for instance, John Chubb and Terry Moe, *Politics, Mar-*

kets, and America's Schools (Washington, D.C.: The Brookings Institution, 1990).

16. John Witte, "Choice and Control: An Analytic Overview," in *Choice and Control in American Education*, 22.

17. Susan Chira, "Where Children Learn How to Learn: Inner-City Pupils in Catholic Schools," *The New York Times*, 20 November 1991, A14.

18. Personal correspondence, November 1991.

19. Personal correspondence, November 1991.

20. Personal correspondence, November 1991.

21. See Peter W. Cookson, Jr., "The Rise of the Private School: Implications for the Redesign of American Education," 7, and Donald A. Erickson, "Choice and Private School Dynamics of Supply and Demand," in *Private Education: Studies in Choice and Public Policy*, ed. D. C. Levy (New York: Oxford University Press, 1986).

22. A. L. Goldman, "Money Problems Put Some Catholic Schools in Danger of Closing," *The New York Times*, 16 February 1992, A15.

23. Personal correspondence, November 1991.

24. Witte, "Choice and Control."

25. M. Walsh, "Private-School, Religious Groups Join to Back President's Choice Proposal," *Education Week*, 29 January 1992.

26. See James S. Coleman, Thomas Hoffer, and Sally Kilgore, "Cognitive Outcomes in Public and Private Schools," *Sociology of Education* 55 (April/July 1982): 65–76, and James S. Coleman, Thomas Hoffer, and Sally Kilgore, *High School Achievement: Public, Catholic, and Private Schools Compared* (New York: Basic Books, 1982).

27. Anthony S. Bryk and Valerie E. Lee, *Catholic Schools and the Common Good* (Cambridge: Harvard University Press, 1993).

28. For a more detailed discussion of this ideological shift see Cookson, "The Rise of the Private School," 2–4.

29. See the National Center for Education Statistics, *1991 Digest of Educational Statistics* (Washington, D.C., 1991); also, data cited in Cookson, "The Rise of the Private School," 8.

30. Coleman et al., "Cognitive Outcomes in Public and Private Schools," 67.

31. National Center for Educational Statistics, *1991 Digest*, and Cookson, "The Rise of the Private School," 8.

32. See Coleman et al., *High School Achievement*, 43–46.
33. Ibid., 28–46.
34. Coleman et al., "Cognitive Outcomes in Public and Private Schools," 66.
35. Ibid., 69.
36. Ibid., 72.
37. Ibid.
38. Ibid., 74.
39. Coleman et al., *High School Achievement*, 181.
40. Coleman et al., "Cognitive Outcomes in Public and Private Schools," 74.
41. James M. McPartland and Edward L. McDill, "Control and Differentiation in the Structure of American Education," *Sociology of Education* 55 (April/July 1982): 78.
42. Ibid.
43. Barbara Heyns and Thomas L. Hilton, "The Cognitive Tests for High School and Beyond: An Assessment," *Sociology of Education* 55 (April/July 1982): 89–102.
44. Arthur S. Goldberger and Glen G. Cain, "The Casual Analysis of Cognitive Outcomes in the Coleman, Hoffer, and Kilgore Report," *Sociology of Education* 55 (April/July 1982): 103–22.
45. Richard J. Murnane, "Comparisons of Private and Public Schools: The Critical Role of Regulations," in *Private Education: Studies in Choice and Public Policy*.
46. Laura Hersh Salganik and Nancy Karweit, "Volunteerism and Governance in Education," *Sociology of Education* 55 (April/July 1992): 158.
47. Ibid., 159.
48. James S. Coleman and Thomas Hoffer, *Public and Private High Schools: The Impact of Communities* (New York: Basic Books, 1987).
49. Bryk and Lee, "Lessons from Catholic High Schools," 35.
50. Ibid.
51. See Chira, "Where Children Learn How to Learn."
52. Ibid.
53. Bryk and Lee, "Lessons from Catholic High Schools," 2. This paper summarizes the research findings discussed at greater length in their book *Catholic Schools and the Common Good*.
54. Ibid., 7.
55. Ibid.
56. Ibid., 10.

57. Ibid., 12.
58. Ibid., 19.
59. Ibid., 32.
60. Paul T. Hill, Gail E. Foster, and Tamar Gendler, "High Schools with Character," Report Number R-3944-RC (Santa Monica, Calif.: The Rand Corporation, August 1990).
61. Ibid., vii.
62. Ibid.
63. Ibid., viii.
64. Ibid.
65. Ibid., ix.
66. See Milton Friedman, *Capitalism and Freedom* (Chicago: University of Chicago Press, 1962).
67. Ibid., 89.
68. Ibid., 85–98. Also see J. S. Catterall, *Education Vouchers* (Bloomington, Ind.: Phi Delta Kappa Educational Foundation, 1984).
69. See Catterall, *Education Vouchers*.
70. Ibid., 20.
71. Ibid., 21.
72. Ibid., 22.
73. See Amy Stuart Wells, "Experiment Pioneered the School Choice Concept," *The New York Times*, 22 August 1990, B6.
74. Ibid., and see Catterall, *Education Vouchers*, 31.
75. J. S. Catterall, *Tuition Tax Credits: Fact and Fiction* (Bloomington, Ind.: Phi Delta Kappa Educational Foundation, 1983), 15.
76. Ibid.
77. Congressional Quarterly Almanac, vol. 28, 97th Congress, 2nd sess. (1982); vol. 39, 98th Congress, 1st sess. (1983); and vol. 40, 98th Congress, 2nd sess. (1984) (Washington, D.C.: Library of Congress).
78. See Catterall, *Education Vouchers*, 20.
79. Ibid., 22.
80. Ibid., 23.
81. John E. Coons and Stephen D. Sugarman, *Education by Choice: The Case for Family Control* (Berkeley: University of California Press, 1978).
82. See Catterall, *Education Vouchers*, 37–38.
83. John E. Chubb and Terry M. Moe, *Politics, Markets, and America's Schools* (Washington, D.C.: The Brookings Institution, 1990).

84. For a detailed critique of Chubb and Moe's methodology see Valerie E. Lee and Anthony S. Bryk, "Science or Policy Argument? A Review of Quantitative Evidence in Chubb and Moe's *Politics, Markets, and America's Schools*." Paper presented at "Choice: What Role in American Education?"

85. See Chubb and Moe, *Politics, Markets, and America's Schools*.

86. Maria E. Sukstorf, Amy Stuart Wells, and Robert L. Crain, "A Re-examination of Chubb and Moe's *Politics, Markets, and America's Schools*," in *Choice: What Role in American Education?* (Washington, D.C.: Economic Policy Institute, forthcoming).

87. U.S. Department of Education, "America 2000" (Washington, D.C., 1991).

88. Julie A. Miller, "Senate Rejects Private School Choice Proposal," *Education Week*, 29 January 1992, 1, 26.

89. Julie A. Miller, "Reform Measure Dies—Except as Campaign Issue?," *Education Week*, 7 October 1992, 1, 32.

90. Douglas Jehl and Jean Merl, "Bush Outlines School Pilot Proposal," *Los Angeles Times*, 26 June 1992, A22.

91. Ibid.

92. Karen De Witt, "Fanfare and Catcalls for Voucher Plan," *The New York Times*, 24 June 1992, A15.

93. Lynn Olson, "New Approaches: Blurring the Line Between Public and Private Schools," *Education Week*, 7 October 1992, 18.

94. Debra Viadero, "Pennsylvania Senate Approves Sweeping School-Choice Plan," *Education Week*, 4 December 1991.

95. Fine, "Democratizing Choice," 1.

96. American Legislative Exchange Council, *Legislative Update*, 4 (February 1992).

97. See ALEC, *Legislative Update*.

98. William Celis, 3rd, "School-Choice Plan on Ballot in Colorado Puts State in Spotlight," *The New York Times*, 16 September 1992, B7, and Mark Walsh, "Colorado Defeats Voucher Plan, Backs Limits on Taxes," *Education Week*, 11 November 1992, 18.

99. See ALEC, *Legislative Update*, 6, 8.

100. John F. Witte, "The Milwaukee Private-School Parental Choice Program." Paper presented at "Choice: What Role in American Education?," Figure 1, and Carnegie Foundation for the Advancement of Teaching, *School Choice: A Special Report* (Ewing, N.J., 1992).

101. Carnegie Foundation, *School Choice: A Special Report*, 66, and John F. Witte, Andrea B. Bailey, and Christopher A. Thorn, *Second Year Report: Milwaukee Parental Choice Program* (Madison: University of Wisconsin-Madison, Department of Political Science, December 1992), iv.

102. John F. Witte, *First Year Report: Milwaukee Parental Choice Program* (Madison: University of Wisconsin-Madison, Department of Political Science, November 1991).

103. Witte, "The Milwaukee Private-School Parental Choice Program," Table 4.

104. Ibid., 21.

105. Witte, *First Year Report*.

106. Ibid., 10.

107. Ibid., 24–26.

108. Witte, "The Milwaukee Private-School Parental Choice Program," 3.

109. Susan Schacht, "Experiments in School Choice," *Regional Review* (Boston: The Federal Reserve Bank of Boston, Spring 1992), 14.

110. Ibid., 15.

111. Ibid.

112. See ALEC, *Legislative Update*, 10.

113. Schacht, "Experiments in School Choice," 16.

114. Mark Walsh, "Hundreds Turn Backs on Public Schools as Privately Funded Vouchers Take Hold," *Education Week*, 16 September 1992, 1, 18.

CHAPTER SIX

1. Cited in *The New York Times*, "Can Vouchers Hurdle Church-State Wall?" 12 June 1991, B9.

2. See David Tyack and Elizabeth Hansot, *Managers of Virtue: Public School Leadership in America, 1820–1980* (New York: Basic Books, 1982), 77.

3. Joel Spring, *The American Public School, 1642–1990*, 2nd ed. (White Plains, N.Y.: Longman, 1990), 105.

4. N. G. McCluskey, *Catholic Education in America: A Documentary History* (New York: Teachers College Press, 1964), 93.

5. Ibid., 94.

6. See Mark G. Yudof, David L. Kirp, and Betsy Levin, *Edu-

cational Policy and the Law, 3rd ed. (St. Paul: West Publishing Company, 1992), 10–13.

7. Spring, *The American School*, 110.
8. See Peter Cookson, Jr., and C. H. Persell, *Preparing for Power: America's Elite Boarding Schools* (New York: Basic Books, 1985).
9. B. S. Cooper, "The Uncertain Future of National Education Policy: Private Schools and the Federal Role," in *The Politics of Excellence and Choice in Education*, ed. W. L. Boyd and C. T. Kerchner (London: Falmer Press, 1988), 165–81.
10. E. Eidenberg and R. D. Morey, *An Act of Congress: The Legislative Process and the Making of Education Policy* (New York: W. W. Norton & Company, 1969).
11. Cooper, "The Uncertain Future of National Education Policy," 166.
12. Another major stumbling block to the federal government's ability to pass general aid legislation for education was the issue of race and whether federal funds should be spent on legally segregated schools. After passage of the Civil Rights Act of 1964, however, this was no longer an issue, as the federal government was prohibited from supporting racially segregated schools. For discussions on both the race and religious issues see Eidenberg and Morey, *An Act of Congress*, 19.
13. Yudof et al., *Educational Policy and the Law*, 681–83.
14. James D. Anderson, *The Education of Blacks in the South, 1860–1935* (Chapel Hill: University of North Carolina Press, 1988).
15. Lawrence A. Cremin, *American Education: The Metropolitan Experience, 1876–1980* (New York: Harper and Row, 1988), 8.
16. Diane Ravitch, *The Troubled Crusade: American Education, 1945–1980* (New York: Basic Books, 1983), 13.
17. Ibid., 14.
18. Yudof et al., *Educational Policy and the Law*, 681.
19. Ibid., 682.
20. Ibid., 683.
21. For a complete analysis of Establishment Clause cases pertaining to public funds for private schools see Stuart Biegel, "The Legal Pitfalls of School Choice Policy: Protecting Student Rights in a Substantially Deregulated Educational System" (unpublished manuscript). Also see Yudof et al., *Educational Policy and the Law*.

22. Eidenberg and Morey, *An Act of Congress*, 247–48.
23. Ibid., 79.
24. *Lemon v. Kurtzman*, 403 U.S. (1971) 602. Also see Biegel, "The Legal Pitfalls," 2, for a discussion of the *Lemon* test.
25. For a more complete discussion of these cases see Biegel, "The Legal Pitfalls," 6–7.
26. See G. Gunther, *Individual Rights and Constitutional Law* (Mineola, N.Y.: Foundation Press, 1986), 1, 138.
27. See Biegel, "The Legal Pitfalls," 7.
28. *Aguilar v. Felton*, 473 U.S. (1985), 402.
29. Yudof et al., *Educational Policy and the Law*, 136–37.
30. Ibid., 137. Also see P. Lines, "The Entanglement Prong of the Establishment Clause and the Needy Child in the Private School: Is Distributive Justice Possible?," *Journal of Law and Education* 17 (1) (1988), 16.
31. See 473 U.S., 756, 764–65, and Biegel, "The Legal Pitfalls," 8.
32. J. J. Scherer and J. Stimson, "Chapter One Decision Causes Concern, Launches Creative Solutions," *The School Administrator* 42 (9) (October 1985), 17–18.
33. M. Walsh, "Court Backs Rule on Chapter One Religious Schools," *Education Week*, 29 May 1991, 1, 23.
34. *Committee for Public Education and Religious Liberty v. Nyquist*, 413 U.S. (1973), 762. Also see Biegel, "The Legal Pitfalls," 9, and Yudof et al., *Educational Policy and the Law*, 107.
35. 413 U.S., 765, and Biegel, "The Legal Pitfalls," 10.
36. Ibid., 10, and Yudof et al., *Educational Policy and the Law*, 108.
37. 413 U.S., 783.
38. Biegel, "The Legal Pitfalls," 10, and Yudof et al., *Educational Policy and the Law*, 111.
39. *Mueller v. Allen*, 463 U.S. (1983), 391, and Biegel, "The Legal Pitfalls," 11.
40. 463 U.S., 396.
41. 463 U.S., 399, and Biegel, "The Legal Pitfalls," 12.
42. 463 U.S., 403, and Biegel, "The Legal Pitfalls," 12.
43. Personal correspondence, May 6, 1991.
44. Personal correspondence, May 3, 1991.
45. *Witters v. Washington Department of Services for the Blind*, 474 U.S. (1986), 486, and Biegel, "The Legal Pitfalls," 13.
46. 474 U.S., 488, and Biegel, "The Legal Pitfalls," 13.

47. 474 U.S., 488, and Biegel, "The Legal Pitfalls," 13.
48. See Biegel, "The Legal Pitfalls," 2.
49. *Mueller v. Allen*, 463 U.S. (1983), 394.
50. See *Lynch v. Donnelly*, 465 U.S. (1984), 668, 687. Cited in Biegel, "The Legal Pitfalls," 2.
51. 465 U.S., 668, 687, and Biegel, "The Legal Pitfalls," 2.
52. 465 U.S., 668, 687, and Biegel, "The Legal Pitfalls," 2.
53. See L. Greenhouse, "Supreme Court to Rule on Prayer in Graduation at a Public School," *The New York Times*, 19 March 1991, A1.
54. 60 U.S.L.W. 3351 (November 12, 1992).
55. Ibid., 4725.
56. Ibid.
57. For a full discussion of the legal impact of *Lee v. Weisman* on parental choice in education see Biegel, "The Legal Pitfalls."
58. Public Law 101-508 (November 5, 1990). 104 Stat. 1388-233. Chapter 6—Child Care.
59. For a complete discussion on other possible legal strategies see Biegel, "The Legal Pitfalls."
60. Personal correspondence, May 3, 1991.
61. American Legislative Exchange Council, *Legislative Update* 4 (February 1992).

EPILOGUE

1. Fred M. Newmann, "Beyond Common Sense in Educational Restructuring: The Issues of Content and Linkage," *Educational Researcher* 22 (2) (March 1993): 4–13.
2. Ibid., 4.
3. David Tyack, " 'Restructuring' in Historical Perspective: Tinkering Toward Utopia," *Teachers College Record* 92 (2) (Winter 1990): 175–76.
4. Ibid., 177.
5. Ibid., 180.
6. Ibid.